Globalization and Its Impact on People's Lives

2006-2007 Mission Study
with Study Guide

elmira Nazombe

Global Ministries
The United Methodist Church

Cover Photo Credits:

Shrimp
The Source: AP Photo/Judi Bottoni
The Workers: AP Photo/Richard Vogel
The Consumer: AP Photo/Francis Specker

Water
The Source: AP Photo/Debra Reid
The Workers: AP Photo/Williamsport Sun-Gazette, Mark Nance
The Consumer: AP Photo/Thomas Whisenand

Coffee
The Source: AP Photo/Kent Gilbert
The Workers: AP Photo/Esteban Felix
The Consumer: AP Photo/Ben Margot

Cotton
The Source: AP Photo/Betsy Blaney
The Workers: AP Photo/Manish Swarup
The Consumer: AP Photo/Vincent Yu

Globalization and Its Impact on People's Lives, copyright © 2005 General Board of Global Ministries
A publication of the General Board of Global Ministries, The United Methodist Church

ISBN #: 1-933663-01-4

Library of Congress Control Number: 2005936689

CONTENTS

Globalization Timeline: 1940-2005

1940	• FCC rules limit media ownership concentration in radio and TV
1944	• Bretton Woods Agreements create World Bank and Monetary Fund General Agreement on Tariffs and Trade (GATT) established to negotiate rules for trade in goods
1945	• United Nations Charter signed • Dismantling of colonial empires creates independent states in Asia and Africa and neocolonial economic relationships
1947	• Cold War begins pitting capitalism against communism
1948	• Universal Declaration of Human Rights drafted • World Council of Churches founded
1958	• UN Conference on the Law of the Sea discusses resource exploitation of outer continental shelf
1971	• Computer chip invented
1970s	• Global Assembly lines (enabled by dramatically expanded communications due to computers), largely using women's labor, increasingly dominate patterns of production of clothing and manufactured goods • Surplus petrodollars fuel wise and unwise spending/borrowing spree in developing countries
1975	• Advances in computers, fiber optics, satellites, and miniaturized electronics radically alter production and distribution of goods and services and patterns of global investment

1980	• Reagan and Thatcher usher in fundamentalist free market government and free market global economic strategies • President Reagan breaks the air controllers strike, opening an era of diminishing power of unions
1982	• Mexico tells creditors it is unable to pay its debts and the Third World Debt Crisis begins all around the globe as nations are unable to pay escalating debts incurred during the 1970s
1985	• During the UN Third World Conference on Women, women activists from developing countries detail how neoliberal economic policies exploit and hurt women
1986	• World Bank and International Monetary Fund initiate structural adjustment policies in developing countries that promote trade liberalization
1987	• Canadian groups organize opposition to proposed free trade agreement • Free Trade Agreement (FTA) between Canada and U.S. • D.C. District Court eliminates the "fairness doctrine" which outlined the responsibilities of radio and TV owners as public trustees
1988	• Free Trade Agreement (FTA) signed between the U.S. and Canada
1989	• Fall of the Berlin Wall ends Cold War leaving capitalism as single dominant economic system; Transnational Corporations (TNCs) enter former Soviet bloc countries in a push toward privatization
1990s	• Series of United Nations World Conferences dramatically expand the voice of non-governmental organizations in global political, economic, and environmental debates and equality for women • Regional and Bilateral Trade Agreements multiply around the world

Continued...

Globalization Timeline (Continued)

1991	• Worldwide Web created, enabling instant communications around the globe
1992	• North America Free Trade Agreement (NAFTA) between U.S., Canada, and Mexico signed with side agreements on labor and the environment, and in the face of intense resistance from labor, women, environmental, and church groups in all three countries • Maastricht Treaty creates the European Union solidifying economic and political ties between, and expanding number of, European nations west and east
1994	• Free Trade Area of the Americas (FTAA) proposal launched by the U.S. to seek a free trade agreement for all of North, Central, and South America except Cuba
1995	• World Trade Organization GATT adds services, investment and intellectual property rights, and government procurement to trade concerns • UN Fourth World Conference on Women adopts the Beijing Platform for Action outlining governments' responsibilities toward women in the economic, political, communications, and other spheres
1996	• Telecommunications Act engenders further deregulation of media policy
1997	• Hemispheric Social Alliance formed by citizen groups throughout the hemisphere concerned about the FTAA • $1.5 trillion per day of foreign exchange is traded worldwide • Asian financial crisis triggers a global financial crisis when nervous investors rush to withdraw funds from Asian markets; financial speculation becomes a major concern
1999	• 50,000 activists in Seattle protest WTO policies in the first of an ongoing series of activist protests of WTO policies at WTO meetings • U.S. TNCs use illegal accounting techniques to prop up failing profits; Enron, WorldCom, and others collapse in scandal

2000	• Churches, NGOs, activists mobilize around the world on the 50th anniversary of the World Bank and IMF to call for a "Jubilee" cancellation of Third World debts
	• Wealthy countries agree to partial debt relief with terms of more privatization and free trade
	• World leaders gather for UN Millennium Summit, committing to the eradication of extreme poverty and other global social goals by 2015
2001	• WTO Doha Declaration affirms the right of governments to violate trade rules in order to protect the public health of its citizens, while continuing to press for trade liberalization
	• World Conference Against Racism; some Third World nations and activists link colonialism, poverty, racism, and globalization
2002	• Argentina's economic collapse and default on debts; people rebel against economic austerity policies
2003	• World governments and Globalization activists force shut down of WTO deliberation in Mexico
2005	• NGOs and activists around the world join a "Global Call Against Poverty" to urge governments to make trade fair, cancel debts, and address the roots of poverty
	• Central American Free Trade Agreement passed by U.S. Congress expanding the U.S. free trade zone to countries in Central America but not Cuba

Acknowledgements

I would like to acknowledge the contribution of all those who shared their insights and knowledge with me in the preparation of this book, especially: from Fiji, Virisila Buadromo and Shelly Rau; from Michigan, Ada Kidd and Linda Schramm; from Bayou La Batre, Vera Moore and Myra Sutton; and on global communications, Taishi Duchicela, Rajeli Nicole, David Bridell, and Nan Rubin. The stories that they shared are the heart of the story of globalization.

My sincere thanks to all of the 'Elanistas' (economic justice and popular education colleagues): Pam Sparr, Bill Aal, Mariama Williams, Carol Barton, Mary Zerkel, Darlene Gramigna, Susan Williams, Michael James, Jerome Scott, and Walda Fishman, who taught me, inspired me, and generously shared their understanding of globalization and how to make it understandable. This book would not have been possible without them and our history together.

Thanks to my CSR and Women's Division colleagues for their unflagging encouragement through the long months of writing. Special thanks to Lois Dauway for her suggestions that always arrived "right on time," and her flexibility about my work schedule. My gratitude to Toby Gould, Project Manager of Mission Studies, for his helpful advice and strong and practical support throughout the project, and his patience with missed deadlines.

I am deeply grateful to Mae Reed, Administrative Assistant for the Racial Justice Office, for her willingness to take on each research request no matter how obscure. And a very special thank you to my friend Dede Wilson, whose willingness to take on copy editing of the final draft made the completion of the project possible. Also, special thanks go to my son for his support and tolerance for the chaos that this project created in our home.

This book is dedicated to all those working daily for economic justice in the United States and around the world, whose courage and understanding of the realities of globalization present an example to follow and a challenge to people of faith that must not go unanswered.

The Parable of the Good Samaritan

Luke 10

25 Just then a lawyer stood up to test Jesus. "Teacher," he said, "what must I do to inherit eternal life?" 26 He said to him, "What is written in the law? What do you read there?" 27 He answered, "You shall love the Lord your God with all your heart, and with all your soul, and with all your strength, and with all your mind; and your neighbor as yourself." 28 And he said to him, "You have given the right answer; do this, and you will live." 29 But wanting to justify himself, he asked Jesus, "And who is my neighbor?" 30 Jesus replied, "A man was going down from Jerusalem to Jericho, and fell into the hands of robbers, who stripped him, beat him, and went away, leaving him half dead. 31 Now by chance a priest was going down that road; and when he saw him, he passed by on the other side. 32 So likewise a Levite, when he came to the place and saw him, passed by on the other side. 33 But a Samaritan while traveling came near him; and when he saw him, he was moved with pity. 34 He went to him and bandaged his wounds, having poured oil and wine on them. Then he put him on his own animal, brought him to an inn, and took care of him. 35 The next day he took out two denarii, gave them to the innkeeper, and said, 'Take care of him; and when I come back, I will repay you whatever more you spend.' 36 Which of these three, do you think, was a neighbor to the man who fell into the hands of the robbers?" 37 He said, "The one who showed him mercy." Jesus said to him, "Go and do likewise."

Introduction

"The United Methodist Church, as a covenant community committed to God's justice, must work toward a just global economy."

—General Conference Resolution 206.
"Economic Justice for a New Millennium," *The Book of Resolutions, 2004*

"It is time that we manifest gospel values in the economic order. It is after all, our calling."

—General Conference Resolution 208.
"Pathways to Economic Justice," *The Book of Resolutions, 2004*

Continuing a Tradition

Throughout the course of the history of Schools of Christian Missions, The United Methodist Church has turned its attention to issues of the economy. In 1966, we considered issues of *Affluence and Poverty: The Dilemma for Christians*. In 1974, we tried to understand *The Welfare Maze*. In 1988 we explored *The Faces of Poverty in Our Midst;* in the early 1990s we considered *Living Values—Changing Times*, and in 1993, *Global Economics*.

These studies remind us of the long history of public witness by The United Methodist Church in matters of economic justice. In this time of changing realities about wealth and poverty, abundance and scarcity, it is appropriate that we again turn our attention to issues of the global economy.

Goals of the Study

The goal of this study is to explore the places where globalization touches the lives of ordinary people.

The goal of this study is to explore the places where globalization touches the lives of ordinary people. If we are to "manifest the gospel values in the economic order," as a General Conference resolution suggests, we need to understand better where contemporary issues of economic justice touch our lives and where we are faced with decisions about how to act responsibly on behalf of economic justice.

We will examine the impact of economic globalization, including free trade policies, on our lives. We will look at the processes known as outsourcing and offshoring, that is, the expansion of business and corporate operations into many countries throughout the world. We will think about how global media and communications technologies are drastically altering both economic and human relationships.

By looking at these phenomena we hope to understand more fully the impact of globalization on human rights and the social, economic, and political development of various cultures and nations. We will seek to understand the difference between globalization as economic exploitation and the potential for globalization as the development of a global community, one that fosters more intimate contact between cultures and nations. We will try to understand how economically and politically powerful people from different countries often work together for the exploitation of their own people. We will look for spaces of hope: alternatives where people are acting together to build justice, working in concert with others to affirm the vision of global community for each of us individually. We will explore what we as people of faith can do to seek to build a global community based upon justice and solidarity.

In simplest terms, we will place ourselves into the globalization picture. We will look at potential opportunities presented by globalization. We will analyze the changes globalization is making in our lives that may be frightening. To open the door to an understanding of a larger reality, the study will present several specific real-life examples of places where globalization touches our lives.

QUESTIONS TO ANSWER

1. **What is happening** in each local situation? Who are the players? What do they have at stake in the outcome? How are we involved?

2. What is the larger problem? Why does it exist? **What is the connection** between the problem in our community and the problem in communities in other parts of the world? What is the role of global actors in the problem?

3. **What can be done and who will do it?** What actions are already being taken to address this problem? What alternative possibilities can we imagine?

Images of Globalization

It is not easy to separate the economic, social, and cultural dimensions of our lives. The workings of the global economy touch our lives in many everyday places; for example, when we:

- shop at Wal-Mart and notice that almost everything we choose to buy is made in China;

- try to make a long distance call and find that the person assisting us is speaking from India;

- notice that the textile workers at the factory in our town all seem to be immigrant women;

- discover that a transnational corporation has been given a concession to bottle the water that comes from the streams that have always flowed freely near our home;

- find that our friend's job as a medical researcher has been cut by the company because they can pay a researcher much less in the third world and get the same quality of work;

- use the Internet to get directions to drive door-to-door from our house to a job interview with a company two towns away.

The Corporate Globalization box on p. 13 portrays these relationships.

Overview of the Book

In order to focus our attention on seeking globalization through the eyes of ordinary people, each specific discussion will begin and end with stories taken from real life experiences in real communities. We have called these stories **Globalization Times.**

Chapter One, the starting point for the study, is a broad overview of some of the present concerns about globalization through the lens of one specific example from daily life.

Corporate Globalization =

A 16 year old working 18 hours a day for $0.22/hr in Indonesia using toxic glues to make $150 shoes sold by a recently laid-off, non-unionized, part-time worker without health benefits in the shopping malls of America, bought by a teenager using his minimum wage mother's credit card.

Adapted from Polaris Institute, www.polarisinstitute.org

Chapter Two explores the question: How will the natural resources of the earth and from the earth be shared in a way that will provide maximum benefits for individuals, families, communities, and nations? Will we accept the premise that water, oil, natural gas, and other forms of energy are the private possessions of states and corporations and therefore can be exploited for their benefit alone? What is our responsibility to protect and cherish these resources? What rights do people have to access these resources? What of the foods and natural medicines, farmers and traditional healers?

Chapter Three examines a combination of the essential elements of our lives often spoken of with the single word—livelihood. It explores the following question: How will each individual, family, and community have maximum opportunity to build the life that they value; to have decent and safe work with wages sufficient for their lives; to have good health care and other social services; to live in safe communities; and to be able to participate in decisions about their lives in community?

Chapter Four looks at how advances in communications technologies have combined with the values of economic globalization (such as deregulation, privatization, and cosolidation of corporate control) and to jeopardize information as a public resource. It addresses questions such as the following: Who has access to new technologies and who does not? What value messages are the owners of these technologies bringing to us? In the midst of a global media culture that emphasizes competition and celebrates greed, how shall we have space to affirm cultural and religious values that emphasize cooperation, equality, justice, and just mutual sharing and caring?

Chapter Five summarizes the issues and challenges us to consider what response we might make as Christians.

Drawing on Biblical/ Theological/United Methodist and Ecumenical Resources

Each chapter will draw on the richness of our theological and biblical tradition as United Methodists as well as that of the ecumenical Christian family. We have as the compass for this journey the biblical witness of the meaning of God's justice and the statements of The United Methodist Church General Conference on globalization and economic justice.

In particular, the study will focus on the story of the Good Samaritan. This story offers important practical advice about how to live a life of faithfulness. It contains much wisdom about how to deal with the dangers of life, giving instruction in just how far we are expected to go to fulfill the demands of justice. It is also useful as a way to begin to think about building global community since it is the stranger in the story who exemplifies what it means to be faithful. As we seek to answer some of the factual questions about how globalization manifests itself, we will do so in light of these biblical and theological understandings.

A Note on Perspectives

Any time we set out to study complex and conflicting social and economic realities, we bring the sum total of our experiences and our identities to bear on that study. All of us come as people of faith trying to discern and to be faithful to God's action in history. But we also bring to the task our national, racial, ethnic, gender, and class identities. Where those identities are a barrier to our understanding, we will need to try to put our preconceptions aside, at least temporarily, in order to hear different points of view. It is hard to hear our nation or our way of life criticized, but we may need to listen to such criticisms during this study. We may also need to be bold in critiquing ourselves. This is not an economist's study of globalization, it is an inquiry by a person of faith with some experience in working on issues of economic justice and globalization. It is designed for persons of faith who are living in the midst of globalization's many realities.

Alternatives Considered

Throughout our explorations we will always keep in mind our faith responsibility, as well as our opportunity to be involved in building global community. We will ask ourselves what the essential elements of that global community are. What are the things that we as members of a global community need to hold in common? We will explore the idea of a global set of 'common goods'—resources, services, and ways of life that are important to protect for all of us, if any of us are to enjoy them. We will look at some examples of the work already taking place to build and protect the global commons and a global community.

Journaling: Thinking About Our Own Connections

Please take a moment to make a list of some of the things you would like to learn from this study. Make a note of any aspects about globalization that seem to you particularly good—things that affect your own life and the life of your community. You might also want to write down some things that seem very worrying about globalization, things that seem to be threatening to you, your community, and the nation. As we proceed we will continue to relate information about globalization to our own lives and to the major questions that we have about it. Your own reflections will be important to how much you can benefit from the study.

Chapter 1 Globalization Is Connections

"In order to be God's real community, we must realize that people are not here to serve an economic system, but economic systems must serve all people so all live in God's abundance."

—General Conference Resolution 206.
"Economic Justice for a New Millennium," *The Book of Resolutions, 2004*

Globalization Times

DAVOS, SWITZERLAND, January, 2005 — The World Economic Forum, the yearly gathering of rich and powerful persons of the world from both inside and outside government, from business and other sectors, is considering the problem of poverty in the world. The Prime Minister of Tanzania is speaking to the group about children of his country whose lives are threatened by malaria because they do not have mosquito nets. A Hollywood actress wearing a T-shirt with the phrase "God Speeds" on the back, rises and offers to give $10,000 to the government of Tanzania to buy mosquito nets for the children. She challenges others to follow her example and within a few minutes $100,000 is raised to buy mosquito nets for children in Tanzania.[1]

What is Happening?

Globalization comes to us as connections. As a result of experiencing the same or similar economic policies, people from diverse parts of the world feel connected, know about, and sometimes even care about one another. But as this small example illustrates, globalization is also about power and money. As recently as twenty years ago a Hollywood actress might not have been included in this perennial meeting of the rich and powerful people. But one of the outcomes of the growth of citizen voices in the processes of globalization has been the expansion of the conversation table of the rich and powerful, to include representatives of charitable and development organizations as well as interested individuals like the Hollywood actress.

A closer look at this example reveals why it needs to command our attention. These days it is not unusual for the Hollywood actress and those who followed her lead to respond in a genuine way to their concern for the children endangered by malaria. Every day we read news accounts of people making a charitable response when they hear about the problems of people in other countries, so this story is not surprising. We often make this response ourselves, as in the case of the tsunami disaster in December 2004, or the devastation of Hurricane Katrina in September 2005. But these are private responses. The Hollywood actress did not suggest that her government or the other governments had some responsibility for why parents or the Tanzanian government did not have sufficient money to supply mosquito nets for children at risk.

This increasing frequency of a private response to a public problem is a hallmark of the current reality of globalization. It is, in fact, a key strategy of globalization. Those who would promote a particular agenda (often called the neoliberal agenda) for connecting the peoples of the world, believe that private concerns such as corporations, but also non-profit organizations like churches, can do a better and more efficient job of responding to social and economic problems than governments. How many times have we as individuals and as the religious community been asked to make a response to a crisis because it is beyond the capability of government?

The children in Tanzania do not have enough mosquito nets because they live in a very poor country. Their government has been impoverished by a number of things: debts owed to other governments and foreign banks; steadily declining prices for their coffee and other exports; and (World Bank experts would say) too much subsidy of basic services like health and education. Policies determined outside of Tanzania by international institutions like the World Bank and the International Monetary Fund have made a bad situation worse. These institutions establish conditions for the country's access to loans, conditions designed to make Tanzania an attractive location for international investment by dismantling state monopolies and cutting social services.

The story related that $100,000 would purchase 140,000 mosquito nets. Only 2 percent of Tanzanian children under five have mosquito nets while 53 percent are being treated for malaria.[2] This gesture of generosity will have only a small impact on the long-term problem Tanzania faces with regard to malaria. The story did not report whether the Hollywood actress spoke about the need for expanding Tanzania's access to low-cost drugs to treat malaria and development assistance. These strategies would create different environmental conditions, like better access to clean water and good sanitation, which would minimize the incidence of malaria.

The actress' response is an example of one of globalization's key strategies—privatization. Her response of charity is well-intentioned and to be applauded, of course. Children will be helped. It was a gift in keeping with who she is—a citizen of the United States, a beneficiary of a tax system that favors the wealthy person of the economically dominant racial group in her country and in the world. In short, she is a person of privilege. Her response raises several important questions: what is our responsibility and how can it be carried out? Are there ways in which we see ourselves in her actions? Does a private response like this lessen the responsibility to work for systemic change? On the other hand, as we look at this incident from the perspective of the endangered children and their human rights, we might conclude that while these children have on paper (in the Universal Declaration of Human Rights and other international human rights covenants and treaties) the right to life and health, poverty robs them, their families, and their nation of the capability to realize that right. The strategies of economic globalization are bound up in the reasons for their poverty, and those strategies are part of what separates them from the right to life and health and the capability to realize that right. As we continue our exploration of economic globalization we will keep returning to its relationship to human rights and the capability to realize those rights.

Picturing Economic Globalization

The complex reality of globalization is almost impossible to capture in a single image. Throughout the study the following chart (on p. 20) will use the image of a series of concentric circles as a way to think about the interconnections of economic globalization. The chart will include only the major headings. In each chapter it will be up to us to fill in the names of the players involved in each of the basic situations that we will consider.

Reviewing the Elements of Interconnection

Ourselves: In the center we place ourselves. In this center circle we think about three ways in which we might try to view our own life and survival.

1. **Resources:** One-third of the circle is occupied by those things that we need for survival, the products that we use and consume that are necessary to enhance our capabilities for living the

life we value. What things from the natural environment are necessary to sustain our life? Some examples would be water, food, or energy. Economic globalization effects how those things are produced and given away or sold. Every time we look at a particular aspect of economic globalization we will try to think of the resources that are involved.

2. **Livelihoods:** Another third of our circle involves how we ourselves realize our capabilities. Jobs and income, health care, and social supports when we can't help ourselves are also caught up in the economic policies and strategies that we call economic globalization. Each time we look at economic globalization we will have to look at what jobs and whose livelihood is affected by globalization's economic strategies.

3. **Culture and Values:** The final third of our circle has to do with the things that make us a human community, the things that hold us together, such as religion, interaction, and communication.

Advocates: A host of organizations works to protect the rights of individuals and communities. They include organizations created by those directly affected by globalization's economic policies as well as those created to advocate on behalf of others.

Transnational Corporations (TNCs)/Global Corporations: Interacting with the three basic areas in which our capability to realize the life that we value (as symbolized by our human rights) is accomplished, are those institutions and organizations that have an effect on that ability. The next circle portrayed is the circle of the global or transnational corporations or TNCs. We will learn that the global corporation

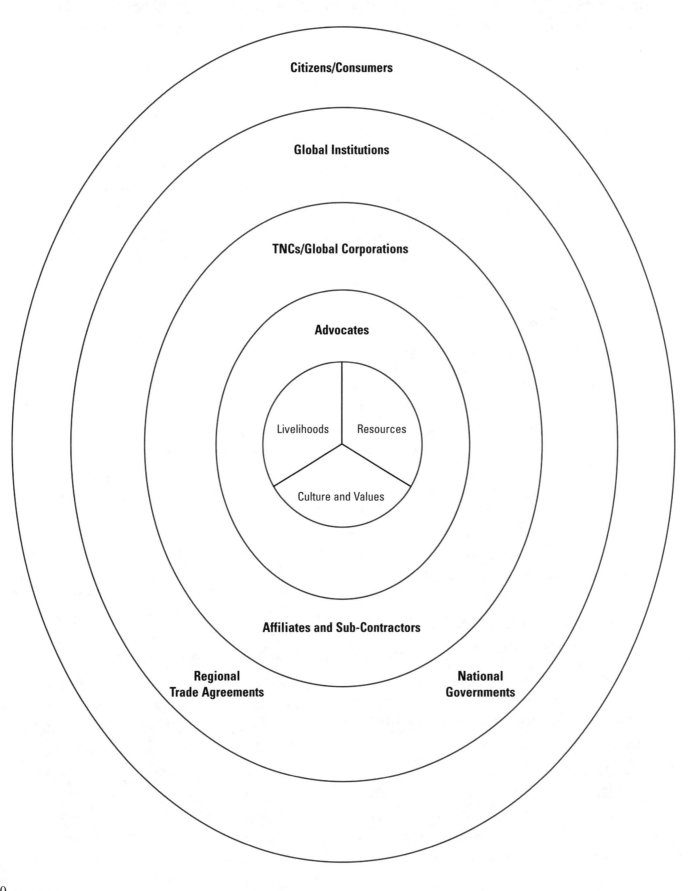

has an array of tools like subcontracting, out-sourcing and offshoring, direct investment, and cross-national partnerships to pursue its own goals of maximizing profits and minimizing costs. Through the wonders of digitized computer technology, the global corporation now has the capacity to scatter its production all over the world. So the corporation has less need for the strict accountability to local or national governments than we might imagine they have or should have. As we look at each situation we will be able to identify the specific tools that corporations are using to pursue their objectives.

Global Institutions: The next circle includes the national and international structures of governance that both enhance and complicate our lives as we try to work to build the life we value. The bottom of that circle is the national governments with differing amounts of economic, political, and military power, as well as local and state governments. Governments have differing philosophies of how to relate to the global corporations. We will be able to identify different government agencies and discover the specific tools that they use to impact globalization, for example, tax policy or government regulation. The government institutions relate to the other half of their own circle: the global governance structures. Well known structures include the World Trade Organization (WTO), The International Monetary Fund (IMF), the World Bank, and a whole host of regional trade agreements like the North America Free Trade Agreement (NAFTA), the Central America Free Trade Agreement (CAFTA), and the proposed Free Trade of the Americas Agreement (FTAA), as well as regional alliances like the European Union. At the heart of understanding the way economic

globalization is currently working is the idea of building a rule-based system for controlling the global economy. The theory is that if all countries are accountable to the same rules for trade, trade will be fair to all. The World Trade Organization is the instrument for developing that rule-based system. In the WTO, 147 nations of the world meet together to agree on rules for trade related to services, investment, agriculture, and intellectual property rights.

Citizens/Consumers: The outside circle is ourselves again in our many different identities as consumers and as citizens. In these identities we interact with the global corporations, the international structures of governance, and even with our own basic struggles for survival. Sometimes these interactions are in harmony with our goals and ourselves, and sometimes they are in contradiction with others and even with ourselves. We will try to determine what tools we may have to act as participants in the building of a just global economy.

Defining Economic Globalization

> "One of our values as Christians is to provide an economy that serves God's vision of abundance to all."
>
> —General Conference Resolution 361.
> "Privatization," *The Book of Resolutions, 2004*

The General Conference described the effects of the global economic system in this way:

…The belief that competition results in greater economic growth underlies much of the emerging global economic order. In the production and consumption of goods, corporations are to compete with corporations, individuals with one another, and societies with other societies. The central value is "more." Greed and the corporate culture of materialism, of "more is better," have permeated our world. It is a culture that has little use for those who lack the means to consume.

—General Conference Resolution 206.
"Economic Justice for a New Millennium,"
The Book of Resolutions, 2004

Economic globalization is a shorthand way of talking about powerful forces that are at work in our world. The manipulation of economic policies and economic opportunities at the national and international level, mainly by transnational corporations and governments, becomes an effort to ensure the domination of certain values in the whole world. Although there are variations in interpretation and execution, there are some powerful dominant values that touch many aspects of present reality. And yet economic globalization values are often in conflict. For example, a stable trained workforce can enhance productivity and the quality of goods produced. This may require decent wages to meet the goal of maximizing productivity. But if the strategy is to minimize costs in order to maximize profit, this can mean looking at wages and benefits as the first place to cut costs. Behind these business practices are fundamental values about workers, communities, and profit. So globalization is ultimately about values.

At stake in this value struggle is the control of nations, economies, resources, and people. Primary actors in the struggle are transnational corporations, international financial institutions, national governments, regional financial bodies, and alliances, all seeking to shape the future. Too often these struggles take place in arenas that most of us only read or hear about through the media. We have not been asked our opinion in any official way. Yet out of these struggles come decisions that affect how much choice our democratic institutions have in making policy on issues like the protection of the environment and access to medicines.

At present, corporations and institutions seem to have rights in the same way that individual citizens have rights. There are those who charge that global institutions like the World Bank, the International Monetary Fund, and the World Trade Organization, whose collective task is to keep the global economy working efficiently, operate to protect these corporate interests. By implication they also operate to advance the interests of citizens in wealthy countries like the United States, where a majority of TNCs are based.

Many people around the world equate economic globalization with the neoliberal model. Liberalism here does not refer to any political ideology but to the economic theory described previously in which the market and corporations are all-powerful. Neoliberals see the market as the most efficient way of organizing an economy to distribute resources, jobs, production, income, wealth, and goods and services. In this framework, the Strategies of Economic Globalization chart outlines four major strategies of neoliberalism, summarizing some of its chief aspects.

STRATEGIES OF ECONOMIC GLOBALIZATION

(Neoliberal Model)

Cheapen the Cost of Production
by driving down living and environmental standards and the quality of social services

Free Movement of Investment Dollars
minimizes the need for corporate accountability to local workers and communities

Create Powerful Global Institutions
more accountable to big business than to citizens

Cut Back Drastically the Ability of National Governments to Regulate Big Business

Adapted from *Economics Education: Building A Movement For Global Economic Justice*, Praxis/Economic Justice Project, American Friends Service Committee, 2001.

The World Council of Churches also noted that economic globalization or neoliberalism:

> …views human beings as individuals rather than as persons in community, as essentially competitive rather than cooperative, as consumerist and materialist rather than spiritual.
>
> —*Policy Reference Committee II Report: Appendix II: Globalization, WCC Assembly*

This means that individual persons and whole communities can become superfluous to the pursuit of the strategies listed above.

We may be tempted to think that we are unconnected to this struggle, able to pass by on the other side of the road as the priest and the Levite did in the story of the Good Samaritan. But we cannot escape our roles. National governments are supposed to act on behalf of us as citizens when they negotiate at the WTO and in other international arenas. Positions taken by these bodies may reflect the perspectives of the corporate sector more than that of ordinary citizens, with a detrimental impact not only in the United States but globally. We have to acknowledge our responsibility as citizens. As consumers, our choice of what to buy and consume links us to workers and producers around the world. It has often been suggested that economics is a set of natural laws governing human behavior, laws such as supply and demand. But economic behavior is the result of human choices. The question we must ask is this: How can citizens reclaim a more meaningful role in these processes that will shape their future? This is both the dilemma and the challenge of globalization.

How can citizens reclaim a more meaningful role in these processes that will shape their future? This is both the dilemma and the challenge of globalization.

Globalization and the Good Samaritan

As we embark on the exploration of the possibilities and contradictions of globalization and our commission to build global community, it is useful to recall the story of the Good Samaritan from Luke 10. Jesus is asked, "Who is my neighbor?" He answers with a story. A man traveling on a dangerous road is attacked by robbers and left for dead. Two officials of the established religion pass him by, but a person of another nationality—a despised race—

stops and cares for his wounds, and then carries him to the nearest town. There this person enlists the aid of an innkeeper and installs the wounded man in the inn. He makes arrangements for the man's care and promises to return and pay for anything additional that is needed. Jesus tells his questioner: "Go and do likewise."

In some ways this story is a metaphor for the reality of economic globalization. Both in the United States and all around the world, many have been figuratively and literally robbed and left for dead by some transnational corporations and other forces of economic power. Many of those who are supposed to give aid have chosen to pass by on the other side. Perhaps it has been too easy for some of us to identify with the Samaritan. But we are more firmly identified with those officials of the established religious community. Perhaps we have not experienced being the "other," offering assistance even though we have been the despised. But if we contemplate our challenge to build global community, our job is perhaps more complicated than that of the Samaritan. A seminary professor once said, "How do we love our neighbor, when our neighbor is the neighborhood?" Globalization has made our neighborhood the whole world in a very real and immediate sense. This study is about how we go about loving that neighborhood, responding as the Samaritan did.

> "The community provides the potential for nurturing human beings into the fullness of their humanity. We believe we have a responsibility to innovate, sponsor, and evaluate the new forms of community that will encourage development of the fullest potential in individuals."
>
> —Social Principles ¶161, II,
> *The Book of Resolutions, 2004*

> "We affirm all persons as equally valuable in the sight of God. We therefore work toward societies in which each person's value is recognized, maintained, and strengthened."
>
> —Social Principles ¶162, III,
> *The Book of Resolutions, 2004*

These words from the Social Principles challenge us to think about globalization in a particular way. Could globalization represent a new possibility for community, one that is global in scope? If so, then in order to "encourage development of the fullest potential," how do we handle our responsibility to innovate, sponsor, and evaluate? What insights and critical perspectives do we need to help us assume responsibility for working for a vision of global community? Globalization is about more than possessions and power and money. At its heart, globalization is about values. As people of faith our values require that we respond with caring for Tanzanian children in need. Our values mandate that we say "No" to the idea that the lowest possible wages and minimal safe working conditions represent an opportunity to

> "…Worldwide, poverty and hunger has increased, especially among women and children. Human rights have become untenable…some one billion workers, one third of the world labor force, remain unemployed or underemployed….Many corporations have shifted to the use of temporary and part-time workers in order to avoid paying benefits… the international stock markets and corporate traders are not accountable for the wages and workplace conditions of workers…"
>
> —General Conference Resolution 206.
> "Economic Justice For a New Millennium,"
> *The Book of Resolutions, 2004*

use poverty as a competitive advantage for poor communities and nations to foster development. Therefore as people of faith led by the spirit of the Gospel, we may find in globalization opportunities to advance the vision of the spirit of peace and justice and dignity for all, "encouraging the fullest potential in individuals."

But we know that globalization is not only about new possibilities; it is also about exploitation and greed. We see that globalization is both about possibility and about danger. What tools do we have to help us consider our course of action?

> "We are challenged to globalize an ethos that respects and protects human life with human rights so that all 'may have life, and have it abundantly' (John 10:10b) as God intends."
> —General Conference Resolution 309. "Globalization and Its Impact on Human Dignity and Human Rights," *The Book of Resolutions, 2004*

Human Rights and Capabilities

The General Conference Resolution, "Globalization and Its Impact on Human Dignity and Human Rights," encourages us to view globalization through the lens of human rights. The resolution recommends to us these words from Kofi Anan, General Secretary of the United Nations:

> Human rights are what make us human. They are the principles by which we created the sacred home for human dignity. The human rights are what decency requires and conscience commands.[3]

Is this not another way of speaking about how to have life and to have it abundantly? Human rights can be a tool to help us think about how persons and communities can, in the words of the Nobel Prize winning economist, Amartya Sen, "...lead a life that they value."[4]

> Capabilities are those things that enable people to fully claim their rights.

But is it enough to declare that rights exist? In the story about the Tanzanian children, it is clear that they have a right to live a healthy life but little possibility of being able to exercise that right. The response of the international community at Davos was a response of charity, not a response of rights. How might those Tanzanian children be empowered to claim their right to life and health in a way that includes the full possibility of its achievement? Sen has suggested that it is important to go beyond the declaration of rights and look at those conditions under which those rights can be realized. He calls those conditions "capabilities." Capabilities are those things that enable people to fully claim their rights. If I have a right to health but live in a system that requires me to purchase health care and I have no money, I lack the capability to claim and exercise that right to health. That's the reality of the Tanzanian children who contract malaria for lack of mosquito nets. The idea of *capabilities* suggests that we need to look at policies and situations and ask the questions:

• Do they curtail or enhance a person's or a community's ability to live an abundant life?

• Do they expand or contract discrimination and inequality based upon race, gender, class, age, and other identity factors?

• Do certain policies privilege one kind of right or one person over another, or support one kind of right while ignoring another?

If the mosquito nets help the Tanzanian children claim their right to a healthy life, but the economic conditions in their communities mean that they don't have enough food to eat, then we have only partially succeeded in helping them to realize that right.

This point leads us to another important understanding about the tool of human rights; it is that human rights cannot be separated. The General Conference resolution puts it this way:

> The indivisibility of human rights underscores the understanding that freedom is hollow without food, that justice without jobs is like a clanging cymbal, and that liberty is a sham when people do not have land to inhabit and to farm.[5]

Another value perspective may be helpful to us as we turn our attention to trying to understand globalization or other insights from the General Conference Resolution 309 on Globalization and Its Impact on Human Dignity and Human Rights.

> Human dignity is the common bond that affirms the individuality of each human being while celebrating the plurality and variety of communities to which each belongs, including the diverse economic, political, religious, ideological, racial, class, gender, and ethnic identities each represents.[6]

If there is a common bond among people, then the realization of abundant life is not an individual affair. If in fact our neighbor is a neighborhood, that is, the whole of the planet, then we must judge economic strategies in their ability to affect everyone. We are familiar with Jesus' call for us to look out for "the least of these," the most vulnerable. But is this enough? How we are connected to the least of these is a question of how we work to find the promise of abundant life for the whole of humanity. Does this mean that we need to think about the things that we hold in common? Is there such a thing as the common good? Our faith tradition also calls upon us to be faithful stewards of God's creation. As we go through our exploration of globalization and its impact on our lives, we will use the yardstick of measuring the impact of policies on both the most vulnerable and on the common good. We will try to discern what needs to be protected for the whole of humanity.

There is no escape—global economic, social, and cultural processes involve all of us. The success or the failure of the positive and negative forces in globalization will impact not only our future, but the future of our children and of our children's children. Can we discern and join the spirit of God at work in the world today in the midst of these processes?

Chapter 2 Global Resources

All creation is the Lord's, and we are responsible for the ways in which we use and abuse it. Water, air, soil, minerals, energy resources, plants, animal life, and space are to be valued and conserved because they are God's creation and not solely because they are useful to human beings.

—Social Principles ¶ 160, I.
"The Natural World," *The Book of Resolutions, 2004*

The natural world provides much that makes our life possible. Over countless centuries rich supplies of minerals, oil, and natural gas developed that we now convert into energy and essential products. But the natural resources of the planet are in many cases finite. At the end of the last century it became clear that we have been using them up at an alarming rate—so quickly, in fact, that many of these resources are now in danger of being entirely depleted.

Over the centuries farmland with rich fertile soil has produced the foods that sustain our bodies. Societies have linked their cultures to the foods they eat. Harvested seeds have provided the source for continued survival. Small farmers and farming communities have traditionally been the core of many societies. It is in this context that we must examine an emerging global value that suggests that these resources are all for sale, that access to these resources and the ability to use them should be linked solely to ownership and the ability to pay. This value is over against the reality that the lives of people in all countries depend on these resources.

So imagine this situation: To gain the economic resources to buy manufactured goods or food, a country may find it necessary to sell its gold or its copper, its oil, its coffee, or the rights to portions of its land. Because a country may lack technology or capital, its leaders must invite others in to develop these resources. Consider the following:

- What happens when a country wants or finds it necessary to sell, for example, its water? Can its citizens today and future generations do without water?

- What happens if the country and its people lose control over water resources and outside individuals and corporations can decide who has enough to drink and who goes thirsty, how quickly natural water reserves are depleted or become polluted?

- Who controls the water supply in your community? Has control effectively shifted to private hands?

- Are there any rules about the control of essential life-giving resources? Who makes those rules? Who can have a say in changing those rules?

In this chapter we will use the example of water because it is such an elemental resource, and because future generations may judge our efforts to build a global community based on our handling of the control of water.

Take a moment to make a list of some of the resources of the natural world that are critical to your life, resources that you use every day and perhaps take for granted. As we learn more about globalization and the control of resources, we will explore how globalization is affecting each item on your list. Does your list include water, natural gas, electricity, and food? Keep this list handy—you will want to come back to it later.

Globalization Times

BIG RAPIDS, MICHIGAN — "Water must stay under public domain; if it is allowed to be under private control there been no conservation and poor people won't be able to afford it," declared Lois Hartzler, United Methodist Woman from Wideman, Michigan. Ms. Hartzler is among citizens of Mecosta County Michigan who formed Michigan Citizens for Water Conservation to express their concern for the extraction of 720,000 gallons of water each day by Nestlé Waters, a subsidiary of the French-owned multinational Nestlé, and sold under the name Ice Mountain. The water comes from Sanctuary Springs, a shallow aquifer that ultimately feeds into Muskegon River and Lake Michigan, part of the Great Lakes that contain close to 20 percent of all the freshwater on earth.

The company promised to provide as many as two hundred jobs in this area of high unemployment. In return the company received permits to dig wells, a $9.5 million tax break, and a twelve-year reprieve in paying property or school taxes. Nestlé continues to buy land in Michigan for future use in bottling water if the company's current bottling is profitable.

United Methodist Women in Michigan were among citizens challenging the company.

Citizens' groups note that Michigan has no clear authority to regulate underground water unless it is a health threat. County residents are concerned that extracting the water is harming wetlands, lakes, and streams. Privatization of water, selling of water, water rights, public trust, and water diversion are being debated in many arenas.

With the help of Mrs. Hartzler and a small number of residents on a limited budget, two couples filed a suit against the water bottling company. One attorney represented the residents while nine attorneys represented the corporation. In November 2003 Judge Lawrence Rood handed down an order for Nestlé to stop extracting the spring water. The judge found that Nestlé's pumping resulted in an approximately two-inch drop in the surface level of the stream, causing area wetlands to lose up to 75 percent of their open water and local lake levels to fall by up to six inches. The court ruled the diversion and sale of groundwater that diminishes or harms the waters of the state's lakes and streams is harmful. He stated that permits issued by the state were based on inaccurate, incomplete, and flawed reports. Nestlé appealed and was granted an emergency stay and permission to continue pumping. The *Continued...*

state government supported the ruling in order to maintain jobs and to allow the development of water policy.

In 2004 the West Michigan Annual Conference passed a resolution to continue its support of citizens' action on this issue, calling for a boycott of bottled waters sold by the Nestlé Corporation, including Ice Mountain, Perrier, Poland Spring, and eleven other brand names. The Conference Board of Church and Society was commissioned to send notification to Michigan Governor Jennifer Granholm urging her to pursue comprehensive legislation whereby fresh water cannot be bottled and/or sold for profit without a public process to determine its sustainability and its environmental, economic, and social consequences.

Vicki Sladeck, United Methodist Women mission coordinator for social action for the district, summed up the position of United Methodist Women: "We decided to make this issue a priority because not only is this a local happening but it affects the world." In a close vote, the 2005 Western Michigan Annual Conference declined to renew the boycott resolution, citing lack of effectiveness of the boycott and the impact on local jobs.[7] ■

The Story of Fiji Water

Half a world away another community also faces some interesting issues related to the bottling of water. Fiji Water Company is a U.S.-based company that is currently bottling water for sale internationally using an ancient aquifer located on indigenous communally owned land in Fiji.

Globalization Times

WASHINGTON, DC, October 2004 — "For nearly a decade, this company has done a lot more than bottle water in the South Pacific. Fiji Water has reached out to communities all around the island and helped them to meet their most important social needs," said outgoing Secretary of State Colin Powell as he presented the 2004 Award for Corporate Excellence to David Gilmore, Canadian billionaire, co-founder of the company known as Fiji Water. The award recognizes U.S. firms for outstanding corporate citizenship, innovation, and business practices. Fiji Water is the second largest imported bottled water seller in the United States. Its sales in 2002 were $40 million.

These revenues make it Fiji's largest selling export. Fiji Water is sold in the United States, Canada, United Kingdom, Australia, Mexico, the islands of the Caribbean, and the South Pacific.

Fiji Water operates on the basis of the 20-year lease agreement with the traditional indigenous communal owners of the land. The company has created a trust fund that has so far provided $300,000 for capital improvements to the villages in the area. These improvements include water and sanitation systems and improvements for churches and civic buildings. In addition to this, the company employs one hundred people, according to

Continued...

their website, "...many of whom had never been employed on a full-time basis."[8] In addition the company has built five feeder kindergartens and provided scholarships that have enabled two local teachers to obtain certification and employment by the Ministry of Education of Fiji.

Indigenous landowners have expressed satisfaction with their association with the company. They say their children have been able to get better education because they get a subsidy from Fiji Water, and significant improvements in their standard of living have resulted. In fact, this kind of investment partnership is being hailed as the kind of model that should be used widely. The Fiji Water website does promote the virtues of its partnership but does not appear to give the same message inside Fiji.

Some landowners point out that land in Fiji is owned by communal groups, and the communal groups can involve a number of villages; however, the benefits from the Fiji Water project have only been for the particular village that is closest to the Fiji Water site.

Promotion and oversight of investment are the responsibility of two Fiji government bodies: the Fiji Institute of Trade and Investment and the Native Land Trust Board. The Native Land Trust Board, a government agency that has been in existence since independence, set the terms of the lease for the site of the bottling plant. It is charged with the responsibility of protecting the interests of indigenous people with regard to land, minerals, and other natural resources. A Fiji human rights activist explained that the Fijian communal land ownership system makes it difficult for an individual within an indigenous group to work on behalf of the group to carry out such an investment effort, because the group must act in concert. Therefore it is easier for an outsider to take the initiative to develop the land than for a local Fijian. She added, "Whether or not the indigenous people who are involved are fully consulted or are aware of all of the implications, that is questionable."[9]

A locally owned bottling company attempted to open a bottling plant in a nearby area using the same water source. The locally owned business was held up for several years in litigation with Fiji Water over the issue of trademark name. The local company is now selling water for the local market. A local activist noted: "They don't use the same bottle, they don't use the same name, but it is the same water that is coming from Fiji Water. It is interesting because it is a local company and they are locked out because they don't have the marketing dollars, and because they were shut out by an international company like Fiji Water."[10]

Concern has also been raised about the long-term environmental and other impacts on the landowners of having two bottling companies utilize the same water source. Fiji Water alone is extracting 45 million liters of water per year. Again the question is raised: how is government policy balancing environmental and investment goals? Do indigenous landowners have a way to voice their concerns? In 2004 indigenous landowners, feeling that they had exhausted traditional avenues, asked a member of parliament to voice their concerns. The member, a woman, told the Parliament that the government, in its pursuit of trying to encourage investment, was not taking a holistic view of the impact of these investments on indigenous people. Instead of addressing the indigenous concerns directly they challenged her right to question Fijian institutions because she is a woman (in Fijian society women currently have no say in issues of land) and also because she is not a fully indigenous Fijian. The Fiji Women's Rights Movement wrote a letter in support of her statement and her right to speak on behalf of indigenous landowners but commented on the implication of the event: "A non-governmental organization can speak but they really don't, because as in the present case, the powers that be will shut down the way that people are able to speak on behalf of other people like indigenous landowners."[11] ▪

Before beginning the discussion, please take a moment to write down some of your reactions to these two stories:

- What do the experiences of people in Michigan and Fiji tell us about globalization and our interconnectedness?

- Who are the winners and losers in the stories? How are their experiences just one aspect of the global problem of privatization of resources?

What's Happening

Ice Mountain and Fiji Water are just two brands among many in the growing bottled water enterprise, an industry that has annual sales of more than $35 billion worldwide. Bottled water is the fastest-growing segment of the beverage industry, expected to pass milk to become the second most consumed beverage behind soft drinks. More than half of all people in the United States drink bottled water. About a third of the U.S. public consumes it regularly. People say they drink bottled water out of concern about the safety of municipal water. Some say they drink it for the taste; some believe it is healthier than tap water. Others say it's convenient. The claim that bottled water is safer can be challenged because as much as 40 percent of the bottled water is tap water. About 20 to 30 percent of bottled water brands tested contain contaminants. Municipal water sources are highly regulated by the Environmental Protection Agency. The World Wildlife Foundation points to environmental concerns: bottling uses more fuel than water and produces about 1.5 million tons of plastic water bottle waste globally each year.[12]

The experiences of the people of Michigan and of Fiji demonstrate two strategies that are central to how economic globalization functions: investment and private control of public resources or privatization. Economic globalization works to create a climate for international investment. The principles of economic globalization encourage corporations based in one country to seek and take advantage of investment opportunities in other countries. So a Canadian entrepreneur or a French conglomerate is encouraged to build a multi-million-dollar business halfway around the world. The institutions that promote economic globalization encourage governments like the government of Fiji or the state of Michigan to take steps to make their localities attractive for investment with tax incentives and tax breaks. The theory of economic globalization states that economic growth can be fueled by this investment. An additional premise is that if all countries are accountable to the same rules of investment, all companies will be treated equally wherever they are, regardless of their home base. The practice is called national treatment. Under this rule Fiji Water or Nestlé Water, even though they are companies with their home base in another country, must receive the same treatment by governments that a locally based company would receive. According the rules of the World Trade Organization, this is a way to provide equal opportunity for all corporations. The government of Fiji therefore does not have the option of favoring a local Fijian Company to carry out the development of the Fiji national water resource that the aquifer represents. The same is true of the government of Michigan.

Free Trade: The Basics

Consider some of the major areas of our lives that are controlled by global corporations. A primary actor in the drama of economic

New & Revised Map of...
The Corporate World

Owns over 90% of all genetically engineered (GE) crops.

Monsanto, Saskatchewan

Eli Lilly, North America

Boeing USA

"Depends on non-competitive military contracts from the US government for half of its revenues."

Suez Atlanta, USA

Citigroup, USA

United Technologies Colombia

Vivendi Parana, Brazil

Merck, Brazil

Lockheed Martin Chile

GlaxoSmithKline, Ulverston, UK

EADS

'Great global asset swindle.' -see next page

GE Capital, Eastern Europe

Conducts cheap clinical trials.... eleven children died in Nigeria

Nestlé, Togo

Nestlé, Burkina Faso

Pfizer, Nigeria

Nestlé, Ethiopia

Merck, South Africa

Suez Johannesburg

Cargill, India

GE Capital, South Korea

GE Capital, South East Asia

GE Capital, Dabhol Power Plant, India

RWE/Thames Water Jakarta, Indonesia

Tried to hike rates by 35% two years in a row.

WHO'S TAKING OVER?
NO CORPORATE CONTROL

🌾 Food   💧 Water   ✈ Military   💊 Pharmaceutical $ Finance

FOOD

Monsanto: Owns over 90% of all genetically engineered (GE) crops. Suing hundreds of farmers across Canada and the U.S. for saving and replanting Monsanto's seed. One Saskatchewan farmer will defend himself in the Supreme Court of Canada.

Nestlé: World's largest food company. Uses exploitative coffee and cocoa buying policies and GE ingredients. Tried to sue Ethiopia for $6 million in compensation for nationalizing a subsidiary in 1975.

Cargill: Largest private company in the world, one of top world grain handlers. Squeezes farmers by controlling seed markets, grain handling and export. Put small-scale flour processing mills out of business when it entered the Indian wheat market.

Nestlé: World's largest baby milk seller. Markets baby formula to women living in poverty. Consistently violates international code on marketing. Was found giving free baby food samples to health care facilities in Togo and Burkina Faso.

WATER

Vivendi: In Parana, Brazil, the company is getting kicked out for prioritizing profits and dividends over water quality and infrastructure development. Is also mired in lawsuits in the US and France for shareholder conduct under CEO Messier's leadership.

Suez: North American subsidiary United Water got kicked out of Atlanta, USA, in January 2003 for their empty promises about savings, neglecting maintenance work (but charging for it anyway). Boil water advisories were commonplace.

Suez: Trying to squeeze the poorest of their last cent for a profit, Suez is installing pre-paid (automatic cut-off) meters in the poor townships of Johannesburg and hiking water rates.

RWE/Thames Water: Tried to hike rates by 35% two years in a row for dirty water in Jakarta, Indonesia. The company has been met with consumer protests, strikes, and lawsuits over unfair contract awarding practices connected in the Suharto regime.

PHARMA

Pfizer: Conducts cheap clinical trials in Southern countries. During one such trial, eleven children died in a Nigerian epidemic camp. Thousands protested, demanding Pfizer stop operations in Nigeria.

Eli Lilly: In North America, its Humulin (genetically engineered insulin) has caused severe side effects in thousands of diabetics and over 150 deaths. Refuses to put less harmful animal insulins back on the market.

Merck: A central pusher of patents and high prices for HIV/AIDS treatments. Lowered its prices only after massive international pressure. Lobbies for sanctions against countries producing or importing cheap drugs, such as South Africa and Brazil.

GlaxoSmithKline: Chemical plant in Ulverston, UK is one of the most carcinogenic polluters in the region. In 2001 alone, it emitted 773 tonnes of carcinogens, 10 percent of the national total, in Ulverston. Releases toxins into Ulverston's environment without authorization.

FINANCE

GE Capital: Enormous financial half of General Electric. Finances massive privatization projects, including, along with Enron, the disastrous Dabhol Power Plant in India. Environmental devastation, beaten protesters, and skyrocketing costs were Dabhol's result.

Citigroup: World's second largest financial services company. Manipulated transactions in the USA permitting Enron to hide its true financial condition. Set up complex energy deals allowing Enron to falsely boost its cash.

Citigroup: In Thailand, Citigroup financed a generating company which was built solely to take gas from the Yadana pipeline in Burma. Yadana was built through forced relocation, forced labor, and torture.

GE Capital: 'Great global asset swindle' – bought assets in South East Asia & Eastern Europe at highly undervalued prices. In South Korea, bought out finance companies at rock bottom prices following the Asian financial crisis.

MILITARIZATION

Boeing: As the world's largest builder of civilian and military aircraft, is central to the War on Terror. Demands liberalization of foreign aerospace sectors, but depends on non-competitive military contracts from the US government for half its revenues. CEO Phil Condit is an active player in setting US global trade objectives. Co-chaired the organizing committee for the WTO in Seattle in 1999 with Bill Gates, world's richest man.

EADS (European Aeronautic Defence and Space Company): Generates more than $6 billion in military sales annually, and is a global top-10 arms supplier. EADS executives and ANC members are under investigation for fraud in a $5 billion arms deal with the South African government.

Lockheed Martin: World's largest weapons maker. Annual revenues exceed $25 billion. With US government help, clinched the largest ever weapons sale to South America, for 10 F-16 fighter planes to Chile for nearly $700 million. The deal threatens to spark a region-wide arms race.

United Technologies: One of the top-10 military producers in the USA. Has sold 36 Black Hawk helicopters worth $15 million each to Colombia since 1999, 22 paid for with taxpayers' money through Plan Colombia. The rest were bought by state security forces which have been linked to right wing paramilitaries and the deaths of hundreds of trade unionists and human rights activists.

The time has come to unmask and challenge these corporate agents of the WTO.

Source: www.polarisinstitute.org

globalization is the global or transnational corporation. Many of them are bigger than the economies of many developing countries. They employ workers around the world and exert a broad influence on governments and international institutions. The chart below shows a summary of the realities of the global corporation.

In order to think more deeply about the patterns of investment evident in the examples from Michigan and Fiji, we need to get a better picture of investment around the world. Investment dollars move between countries in the amount of $1 trillion each day. All of this investment is not necessarily for the producing of goods or the giving of services; some of it is just to make money. It is speculative investment in the currency of other countries, or in short-term investments whose main goal is to make profit in a few months or a few days or thirty minutes. So it does not really contribute to the well-being of the persons or the nations in which the investment occurs.

THE GLOBAL CORPORATION

How Many Are There?

- 64,000 TNCs with 866,000 affiliates
- 50% of affiliates are in developing countries, most in Asia
- ⅔ of trade is within companies

TNCs as Employers

- 53 million employed in 2002— most in developed countries

Corporate Tools

- global production line
- decentralized management with instant communication capability
- subcontracting
- outsourcing
- offshoring
- export processing zones
- informal labor market
- financial investments: goods, services, capital

UNDERSTANDING GLOBAL INVESTMENT

How much?

One trillion dollars each day in investment dollars flows—primarily currency and financial transactions but also for production of goods and for services (*that's equal to receiving $100 every second for 317 years*)

Where is it going?

Europe, North American, Japan (*majority*)
Asia, particularly China
Latin America

Who is left behind?

Africa, small island states

What are the benefits?

For each $1 of investment, 30¢ is returned to the investor as profit

What kind of investments?

Telecommunications
Electronic equipment
Petroleum
Motor vehicles
Electricity, gas, water
Media

Who are the largest investor countries?

The Triad: United States, European Union, Japan

Where are the largest transnational corporations?

U.S.: 11
France: 8
Germany: 8
United Kingdom: 7
Japan: 4

But where is the investment going, and what is the balance between investment to developed countries and developing countries? The majority of investment dollars comes from three places in the world: the United States, the European Union, and Japan, and most of it goes back into those countries. In more recent years, however, a larger segment has been going to developing countries. In 2003 China received $53.5 billion in investment. Asia, including China, is the largest recipient of investment dollars in the developing world, followed by Latin America. Africa's share of investment dollars is very small. China's growing role in the global economy is illustrated in the China and Globalization Chart below.

What kind of benefits are the developing countries receiving from these investments, and what did they have to give up? In developing countries, for each dollar of investment, thirty cents goes back to the investor country in repatriated profits. In order to attract serious investment, a developing country in particular will institute a number of government reforms to make its country more attractive to foreign investment. Such reforms might be, for example, changes in rules so that anyone can invest any amount of money anywhere in the country without any restrictions. As a result countries are guaranteed against a nationalization of any of their business assets. Often companies are guaranteed, either openly or under the table, access to labor markets willing to accept the lowest possible wages and lax enforcement of environmental regulations. This might even include stipulations with regard to the right of

CHINA AND GLOBALIZATION

Some Demographics

Total Population: 1.5 billion
Middle Class: 100 million
Graduating Engineers: 325,000 in 2004

Factory for the World

- Assembles more toys, stitches more shoes, sews more garments than any other country
- Largest maker of consumer electronics like TVs, DVD players, and cell phones
- 65% of its exports are from Chinese subsidiaries of TNCs
- Receives $600 billion in foreign investment
- Wal-Mart buys $12 billion in goods from China
- 400 TNCs have research and development work
- Chinese goods save U.S. families $500 each year

Super Market

- 300 million cell phone users, 5 million new users per month, 94 million Internet users
- Motorola, General Motors, and Intel do $1 billion of business
- Chinese consumer can buy five times as much as U.S. consumer in goods and services for same money
- McDonald's has 660 restaurants
- Starbucks has 120 stores
- Microsoft online is joint venture with Chinese government

Sources: "The Chinese Century," Ted C. Fishman,
The New York Times Magazine, July 4, 2004 and www.chinascope.org/en/.

workers to organize. It is important to note that transnational corporations employ 53 million workers outside of their home base countries, so their contribution to global employment is not insignificant.

Understanding Privatization

Historically in the United States and in some other countries, provision of water has been considered a public service. The experiences of the people of Michigan and Fiji are a demonstration of economic globalization's key strategy of privatization. At the heart of the strategy is the idea that private corporations can provide services more efficiently than governments. This concept has made services one of the important new rule-making areas of global trade. In the past, trade in goods, both manufactured and natural products, was the essence of what was governed by international trade rules. With the advent of the World Trade Organization, countries of the developed world that are the home base for many large transnational corporations, have pressed for and succeeded in having international trade in services included in the discussions. The resulting new rules, called the General Agreement on Trade in Services (GATS), includes some 43 services, including health care, insurance, child care, water and waste management, welfare delivery, highways, transportation, passports, and others. Citizens of the United States have long considered such services a part of the system of public utilities and services. Transnational corporations have been eager to open up lucrative markets in the service areas in other developed countries, but also in the developing world.

The Trading Services Chart (p. 38) outlines the major aspects of that treaty. As the discussion of privatization proceeds, refer to this chart to see how the actions of government and corporations are covered under the treaty. The WTO will be discussed in more detail in the next chapter.

The bottling of water is just one of the ways in which water can be privatized. Another form of the privatization of water is through the takeover of the oversight and management of public water systems by private corporations. As the Water Privatization Picture (p. 37) illustrates, two global corporations operate and manage water systems in 130 countries and service 110 to 115 million customers. There were 100 private takeovers of water systems between 1990 and 1997. The United Kingdom has completely privatized its water system and many countries in the developing world are being urged by the World Bank and the International Monetary Fund to do the same. World Bank structural adjustment programs included privatization of public services as a part of their loan conditions. In 2000 the International Monetary Fund made 12 agreements with developing countries that included water privatization as a condition for the receipt of loans. It is clear that some countries may choose privatization because they see that as the best strategy for development, and others have it chosen for them.

WATER—PRIVATIZATION PICTURE

The State of the Global Commons

Available Water

- 70% of the earth is water
- 97.5% is salt
- by 2025 ⅔ of the people of the planet (52 countries) will be facing water stress

Who's Thirsty/Who Can Afford to Drink

- Urban Poor pay 12 to 100 times more per liter
- In Detroit: 40,752 homes cut off for non-payment to privatized water company
- ½ of all people in the U.S. drink bottled water
- ⅓ drink bottled water regularly

Safe Water

- 1.2 billion people have no access to safe water
- 2.4 billion people have no access to adequate sanitation
- 5 million die of water related diseases
- 2.3 billion die of diseases related to dirty water
- 40% of bottled water is tap water
- 20-30% of bottled water is contaminated

Privatization—Alternate Routes and Impacts

Private Ownership and Management of Public Systems

- rate increases
- water shut-offs for non-payment
- poor service
- loss of tax revenue

Bottled Water

- 50% of people in the U.S. drink bottled water
- 40% of bottled water is tap water

- 20-30% of bottled water is contaminated
- bottled water uses 1.5 million tons of plastic
- bottled water is the 2nd largest drink industry in the U.S.
- tap water costs .001% of the price of bottled water
- bottled water depletes stretched fresh water resources and degrades the environment through aquifer mining

Global Water Power Realities

Global Managers

- two companies, Veola and Suez, operate in 130 countries with 110-115 million customers
- other companies involved are Bechtel, Andrews, and formerly Enron
- there were 100 private takeovers of water systems between 1990-1997
- World Bank estimated the value of water management business to be $10 trillion

The Big Bottlers

- Nestlé: 77 brands including Perrier and Poland Springs
- Coca Cola: Dasani and others accused of causing water shortages

- Pepsi: Aquafina, the most popular brand in the U.S., is from tap water

Global Policy Advisors

- World Bank Structural Adjustment programs included privatization of public services
- International Monetary Fund in 2000 made 12 agreements with developing countries that included water privatization as a condition of loans

Trying to Make a Difference

Millennium Development Goal 7: halving the proportion of people without safe drinking water by 2015

TRADING SERVICES (PUBLIC, NON-PROFIT, CORPORATE)

Rules

- Irreversible market access
- Equal treatment regardless of social, labor, or environmental issues
- No unnecessary barriers due to domestic regulations
- National treatment for foreign-based countries
- Military expenditures exempt from WTO rules

Affected Services

- Health care (hospital, home, dental, child, elder)
- Education (primary, secondary, post-secondary)
- Museums, libraries, law, social assistance, architecture
- Energy, water service, environmental protection, postal service, transportation
- Insurance, tourism, real estate, publishing, broadcasting

Coverage

Legally binding contracts for all governments who sign, and applicable to all areas they designate

Enforcement

WTO Trade Sanctions

What's the Problem?

Now that we have described the local situations and also seen some of the global players, we are better equipped to think about how we might make a faithful response to these realities of economic globalization. Local economies are often very vulnerable: employment opportunities may be limited, unemployment may be high and businesses may be facing competition from other states, cities, and countries. Into this environment comes the transnational corporation with funds to invest, looking for the most profitable opportunities. Under these circumstances governments, both local and national, may see investment as the best possibility for meeting their responsibilities.

Another part of the problem is the weakening of the oversight role of local and national governments. During the last decades pressure for less and less involvement of government in the lives of citizens and businesses has been almost overwhelming. Government budgets at all levels have continued to be scaled back and as a result the regulatory function of govern-ments has been diminishing. It is therefore no wonder that investors find little to deter them in their quest for profits in local places.

Naming Globalization Interconnections for Water Resources
(see chart on p. 39)

To help us think about the two situations, take a moment to fill in the Globalization Interconnections chart. The chart is one way to think about the interactions of the various players in the two situations: local people, local and national governments, global corporations, and ourselves as citizens and consumers. On the chart, list some of the players in Fiji and Michigan. List some of the economic needs and differing cultural and historical realities that conditioned the responses of the local communities. List the global corporate actors who were involved. Was there a role being played by the global institutions?

see instructions on p. 38

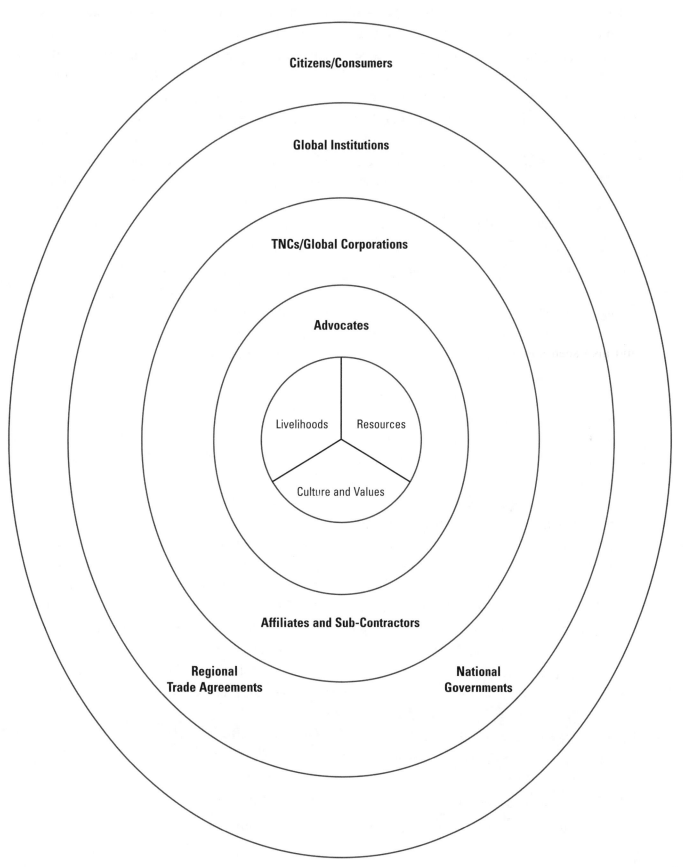

There are a number of players from the local to the global level involved in the drama of water and the right to water. We have seen local communities on two sides of the world struggle to assert their right to some control over the use of water from their community. We have seen national governments and state governments carrying out their understanding of their responsibilities for the regulation of water and for development and prosperity of communities. We have seen the international corporations reaching out to investment in these communities to create profitable businesses and business climates for themselves. We have learned a little about the global institutions known as the World Trade Organization, the World Bank, and the International Monetary Fund. These institutions, in fulfilling their role of management of the global economy, have encouraged transnational corporations to invest around the world as well as encouraging the process of privatization of public resources. So each of the actors has a different kind of stake in the provision and access and profitability of water.

How are we engaged? What is our involvement in this reality? As we saw from the chart, more than half of the people of the United States drink bottled water and one-third of them do it on a regular basis. Communities in Detroit and Atlanta and other places are struggling with the privatization of public water and waste treatment systems. Probably many of us are in communities where city and state governments are struggling to attract investment in order to bolster flagging local economies. There is little question that all of us are touched by economic globalization and strategies for investment and privatization.

In both Fiji and Michigan a common resource is at stake. Who will ultimately control the future of that resource? In Fiji, by law the indigenous community possesses the right to their land and its water resource. But what is their capability for using that resource to enhance their possibility of leading the life that they value? They do not have the economic power to fully develop this resource for their own benefit. WTO rules say that their government cannot give a local company preference over a transnational corporation for the development of that resource. In both communities the control of environmental resources is intricately bound up with the economic demands of the community. Communities are being asked to choose between the control and protection of environmental resources and ceding the control of those resources to others in order to further and strengthen economic benefit to citizens within the community.

What Can Be Done?

Communities around the world are facing problems similar to those in Fiji and Michigan. What is to be done and who will do it? Or, as the Gospel writer asks, who is my neighbor? How can we go and do likewise, following the example of the Good Samaritan? Let's imagine ourselves and our own community or communities that we know. Use the Negotiating the Global Commons Worksheet (p. 41) to organize your reflections on how to respond to these issues around the four major topics discussed so far. Following are some of the questions that will need to be answered.

Where Globalization Intersects with Communities:

• What are the basic resources that we need for life in our communities?

• Are any of these resources endangered?

NEGOTIATING THE GLOBAL COMMONS: RESOURCES

Investment:

Privatization:

Democratic Control:

Resources at Stake: Water, Food, etc.:

• Remember your original list of the resources that are vital to your life and the life of the community. What's happening with water? What about food or electricity or other sources of power within your community?

• If your community and its needs are "bleeding on the side of the road" as in the story of the Good Samaritan, what would it mean to put yourself in the shoes of the Samaritan?

• Are there groups already at work challenging negative aspects of globalization in your community? Or are the priests and the Levites working to support the kind of processes of investment and the ceding of the control of natural resources as in the cases that we have just examined?

• Think about the rights you may want to claim for yourself and for others in your community. What about the right to water or the right to food or the right to housing? These are all places within communities where struggles around rights are taking place.

• Try to remember that your neighbor is a neighborhood. What will that mean in this case? Who is acting on behalf of all? Where is the discussion about the common good? Is there anyone in your community talking about claiming rights that will protect the common good? Who is speaking out on behalf of the most vulnerable?

Connecting Rights and Capabilities

• What are the capabilities that are needed in order to put the right to water or food in place in the community?

• Can you draw a picture or make the list of all of the things that would be necessary to insure that any single individual or the community as a whole would be able to have the capabilities necessary to exercise its right to water or its right to food or any other basic necessity?

- What would those capabilities be? Would they include ability to pay that would lead to jobs or other kinds of income supports?

- How does the right to participate in the decision-making process about water or food or other elements of basic necessity figure into the equation?

- What are the connections? How are people in your community who are interested in the right to water or food connected to people in other places? How are they connected to those who produce the food? How are they connected to those who would wish to make a commercial resource out of the water?

- What about those who need jobs? Where is their voice heard? What are the possibilities of interaction with any of these others?

- Where are the spaces in which government responsibility to act on behalf of its citizens happens? Who influences governments? To whom do governments listen? Who are the powerful and who are the powerless?

- What investment strategies does your local government have? What is the connection between political power and economic power in your community? What positions do your elected officials take concerning oversight of business or corporate interests? If there are trade-offs to be made between jobs and the environment, what will be the guiding values?

- What would it be like if the resources that are spent on the luxury of bottled water went to support provision of safe water for all in the United States and around the world?

The examples from Michigan and Fiji illustrate that a vital component of life in the world of globalization is the effort now being made by local people to assert their rights. Other people in other places are also trying to take control of situations created by globalization. Many are mobilizing to act on behalf of the rights and capabilities of people, indeed to take some steps toward building a global community. Action is taking place on several levels:

- People are looking at their own lives and trying to think about whether there are changes they can make in their own way of doing things that might contribute to more global change.

- As people work to revitalize the accountability of government to its citizens at the local level, they are also looking to national governments to make declarations affirming fundamental rights.

- Activists are working at the global level and on global institutions like the WTO in the World Bank, trying to secure changes in their policies.

As you will see, the key to positive action seems to be sharing information and ideas. Gandhi is reported to have suggested that we need to be the change that we are working for. Here are some examples of groups trying to be that change.

Water for All Campaign

Beyond reconsideration of your own use of water, and of bottled water in particular, consider joining the Water for All Campaign, which provides research and strategic support to communities around the United States to help them keep their water under local control. Key strategies are making sure that local authorities are providing clean and affordable water to all, promoting locally controlled alternatives to privatization, supporting the human right to safe water, and adequate federal support for water infrastructure. Further information is available at www.wateractivist.org.

A project of the organization Public Citizen, a national public interest group, the campaign includes The U.S. Water Contract Domestic Declaration. The Contract is a statement of principles that opens with these words:

> Water is a common good, the trust of all humanity… Water belongs to the Earth and all species, and therefore must not be treated as a private commodity to be bought, sold, and traded for profit.[13]

The Charter urges the U.S. government to be a party of an international treaty to administer the earth's fresh water supply as a trust.

"Water is a common good, the trust of all humanity. Water belongs to the Earth and all species, and therefore must not be treated as a private commodity to be bought, sold and traded for profit."

You might also want to urge your Conference to study and express support for a Concurrent Congressional Resolution first proposed in 2004 expressing the sense of the Congress with respect to the world's freshwater resources which "affirms water as a public trust and a global good that should not be treated as a private commodity where this would limit or deny public access to fresh water resources." The bill also addresses the issues of water cutoffs and provision of water services as a part of trade agreements and the role of institutions like the World Bank and the International Monetary Fund in giving advice about privatization.[14]

The New Rules Project Institute for Local Self-Reliance

The New Rules Project believes that local communities matter. This national non-profit research and education organization based in Minneapolis provides resources for activists, policy makers, and organizations looking for innovative public policies that have been enacted around the world that could be used to make local communities vibrant and strong. It calls for developing principles of "new localism":

1. Decisions to be made by those who will feel the impact of those decisions;
2. Communities accepting responsibility for the welfare of their members and for the next generation;
3. Households and communities possessing or owning sufficient productive capacity to generate real wealth.

The project encourages exchange of information on local initiatives in ten different sections: agriculture, electricity, environment, equity, finance, governance, information, retail, sports, and taxation. For example, if you are interested in equity issues, you can learn more about local initiatives around providing livable wages, health care, and education to all citizens. The website features information and real experiences from different places (local, national, and global) on these sectors. If you have a question about a local problem you can email "Dr. Dave" at drdave@ilsr.org.

Corporate Social Responsibility

Agribusiness Accountability Initiative of the Center of Concern, a religious think tank based in Washington, DC, has created an open and ongoing forum for sharing research, advocacy ideas, networks, and public education strategies. It seeks to address the disproportionate impact of transnational agro-food companies and retailers on the livelihoods and food security of farmers, workers, consumers, and communities around the world. One strategy is to work with investor advocacy organizations and socially responsible investment firms to design and implement an engagement strategy with agribusiness. The initiative is hosting events across the United States in cities like Chicago and Kansas City, as well as in London, Brussels, and Sao Paulo, Brazil. The events are bringing together over three hundred civil society leaders in more than thirty countries to share analysis of food industry issues, support each other's reform efforts, and create new cross constituency research and advocacy.

Sign of Hope: Methodist Youth and Water and Gas Wars in Bolivia

Gustavo Adolfo Ali Alarcon is a student of economics at the University of St. Andrew in La Paz, Bolivia. He works as the National Coordinator of the Methodist Youth Federation in Bolivia. The Federation works on training and capacity building for youth leaders and has focused its attention on two trade agreements that are harming Bolivia: the North American Free Trade Agreement and the Free Trade for the Americas Agreement. This is his story of globalization and resources in Bolivia.

In our country, because of poverty and the unjust distribution of economic resources, social and union movements have grown up to defend natural and energy resources of our country. Since 1985, Bolivia like other countries of Latin America, has experienced the implementation of the neoliberal economic model of globalization. This model makes a way for powerful transnational forces interested only in dominating the world through the exploitation of natural resources and the increase of their own wealth. Through these policies we Bolivians as people of poorer countries of the world have been dispossessed of our inheritance and our resources. We Bolivians are only owners of our water and the air.

The Water War

In March 2000 the government and the city of Cochabamba signed a concession agreement with the Bechtel Corporation, giving it total control of the distribution and consumption of water in the city. Water consumption rates were raised between 30 and 300 percent. According to our culture water is free, but the new policies would prohibit and cut the traditional consumption of water, especially for indigenous people and the poor small farming sector, by placing a price on rainwater consumption. The effect of the imposition of these laws, however, was the growth of a strong resistance aimed at safeguarding the people from these laws. The resistance was known as the Coordination of the Defense for Water and Life. It was a great movement designed to win respect for the rights of citizens and their natural resources and was joined by more than 600,000 men, women, youth, and young adults. They went to the streets for three months in an untiring fight to say "No!" to the imposition of these policies by the government and the transnational corporation. It became a genuine space for the representation of the Bolivian people through continuous protests, meetings, and marches which forced the foreign company out of Bolivia because it had stolen an element vital for all human beings.

Continued...

In 2003 government made an agreement with four foreign companies for the exploitation of 80 percent of all Bolivia's natural gas and its unprocessed exports. Because Bolivia does not have a natural outlet to the sea, a debate arose about whether to ship the natural gas through Chile or through Peru. Social movements interrupted to say "No to the importation of gas from Chile." But as always people's voices were not listened to. But a new demand arose: "No to gas exportation but yes to gas industrialization." In support of this demand a great movement of social activists, union members, and neighborhood people arose to protest constantly against the central government and to ask that its voice be listened to. The response of the government was a military one. Police repression occurred between July and October of 2003. More than ninety people died in the protests, including ten children. The effect of the violence was to create the demand for "the resignation of our president." For more than seven days social and civil movements paralyzed the government headquarters in La Paz and other cities demanding the president's resignation. The president resigned on October 17, 2003, and then peace and calm came back.

The role of the church was very important because we mobilized health equipment and medical support to different regions where there was conflict, and distributed food to families with little resources. In addition a pastoral letter from the Methodist bishops was sent out. Youth played an important role in the movements going to the streets to provide water and food for those who were constant-

ly in the protests, as well as art and cultural events in the public squares, where youth of different ages and cultures expressed their discontent at the death and repression through painting, theater, and dance as instruments of protests. We also had prayer groups that were in our churches with youth and brothers of different religious creeds. We sent two Methodist young adults to the second hunger strike and I personally was in constant communication with the youth leaders to support the hospitals, medical centers, as well as some ambulances. I served as a rescuer of persons who had been shot or hurt brutally by the police and the military.

Individually I felt sad and had a lot of rancor for all the injustices that I saw in those days. It was difficult to contain the tears when we saw many brothers, companions, and friends that were hurt or died. During those seven days no car circulated in the streets and food was beginning to run short but we were all generous and went out into the street to share what little we had with those who did not have anything. This action affected all the neighbors and it was then that everyone took out Bolivian flags and hung them in the doors of people's houses with the black ribbon to show our grief and sympathy, and to signify the indignity for all the assassinated persons. I believe that it is very easy for the government to approve laws in favor of transnationals that violate the political constitution of the state, but if they didn't approve such laws in favor of foreigners the economic benefit would reduce internal fiscal benefits and it would be impossible to govern.

Michigan Postscript

The 2005 Western Michigan Annual Conference *in a close vote declined to renew the boycott resolution citing lack of effectiveness of the boycott and the impact on local jobs.*[15]

An interview with Ada Kidd, environmental activist within the conference, revealed that the issue of bottled water is now taking a back seat to the larger issues of proposals for diversion of water from the Great Lakes. According to Mrs. Kidd, proposals are now being made, supported by water companies like Nestlé, to use the water of the Great Lakes to solve water scarcity problems in western states. Proposals have suggested the creation pipelines or even use of dirigibles to transport water westward.

Meanwhile, the three judge panel that is to rule on Nestlé's appeal met in June, but a judgment may not be reached for two years. Nestlé continues to bottle water and has contracted with a small community to bottle its well water. Linking the two cases is Nestlé's desire to test the application of the Water Legacy Act, which protects the Great Lakes. Although under pressure because Michigan has the highest unemployment rate in the United States, the governor of Michigan has stipulated that water contracted by Nestlé or other water companies cannot be sold outside of the Great Lakes region.

The struggle over the resource of water continues. Mrs. Kidd described the challenges this way: "Citizens and churches, we as people of faith need to look at the picture of the common good for all. What does it mean for our children and grandchildren? How is the environment going to be a viable place to live? We have always used water as an infinite resource. It does matter how we use it."[16] ◼

Chapter 3 Livelihoods

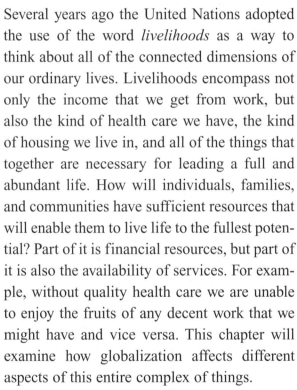

"Work is one way through which human beings exercise their God-given creativity. Scripture also teaches that an economic system should be ordered so that employees receive justice at their place of work."

—General Conference Resolution 237.
"Rights of Workers," *The Book of Resolutions, 2004*

Several years ago the United Nations adopted the use of the word *livelihoods* as a way to think about all of the connected dimensions of our ordinary lives. Livelihoods encompass not only the income that we get from work, but also the kind of health care we have, the kind of housing we live in, and all of the things that together are necessary for leading a full and abundant life. How will individuals, families, and communities have sufficient resources that will enable them to live life to the fullest potential? Part of it is financial resources, but part of it is also the availability of services. For example, without quality health care we are unable to enjoy the fruits of any decent work that we might have and vice versa. This chapter will examine how globalization affects different aspects of this entire complex of things.

For example, let's look at an economic strategy that has affected the lives of many people in the United States and around the world and see how the concept of livelihood helps us understand its implications. This is the strategy of outsourcing.

- What is outsourcing and how does it affect all of our lives? How do the decisions of companies based in the United States to center their production in Asia or Central America affect our ability to have sustainable livelihoods?

- How do free trade and trade deficits and export and import tariffs affect our livelihoods?

- What does it mean to talk about "American jobs?" Should "American jobs" be protected? If so, what are the consequences of this protection for those in other parts of the world who are also part of God's family?

- Or is it possible that the rules of free trade will endanger our access to unemployment insurance or to quality health care? What are the human concerns? Is each individual on his or her own to secure livelihood?

- How will globalization's drive for privatization affect the network of government-sponsored assistance programs to help the poor and those in need? Do the ethics of globalization suggest that if persons are poor it is only because of their own lack of initiative? What about the interconnectedness of livelihoods in different parts of the world? How do we secure honorable livelihoods for all?

Once again, take some time to think about your own livelihood. Think about the elements that are essential to you for living the life that you want to lead. What pieces are intricately intertwined and must come together if you are to have that sustainable livelihood? Make a list of them.

Globalization Times

BAYOU LA BATRE, ALABAMA, December 2004 — "The United States is the most open market for shrimp in the world, but we cannot let Chinese and Vietnamese shrimpers violate the rules of free trade to get ahead of their competition. Dumping is cheating, and we thank the Department of Commerce for offsetting this illegal practice and leveling the playing field for U.S. shrimp fishermen, farmers, processors, and all fairly trading countries."

—Eddie Gordon President, Southern Shrimp Alliance[17]

In 2003 an eight-state coalition known as the Southern Shrimp Alliance, headed by Eddie Gordon, initiated a trade suit charging Vietnam and five other countries with "dumping" shrimp on the U.S. market. The suit concerned two issues: first that Vietnamese exporters were selling their shrimp in the United States at a lower price than the same shrimp sold in Vietnam. Second, they charged that the Vietnamese government, contrary to the rules of the World Trade Organization, was providing subsidies for their shrimp producers. The December 2004 decision upheld this shrimp industry claim and set tariffs for the Vietnamese and Chinese companies up to the level of 95 percent. The organization claims that the illegal dumping of shrimp has put the jobs of 70,000 U.S. workers in jeopardy. Imported shrimp accounts for between 75 and 90 percent of all shrimp eaten in the United

States. Members of the shrimp industry primarily financed the trade suit; however, some funds were received from the government of Louisiana after state officials were convinced of the danger to shrimpers from their state. State funds used were reported to be disaster relief funds from Hurricane Ivan. Additional contributions came from the Mexican shrimp industry that was also suffering from competition with Asian shrimp producers.[18]

The shrimpers' association's (Southern Shrimp Alliance) main opposition was from an alliance of retailers and manufacturers, the Consuming Industries Trade Action Coalition (CITAC), including Toyota and Procter and Gamble, as well as trade groups like the Association of Food Industries. The president of the Boston-based seafood distributor Slade Gorton Company responded that the decision would harm those domestic companies that rely upon a supply of imported shrimp at low prices. He added that it would be American consumers who would suffer the most from the resulting rising prices.[19]

As a result of this decision, persons in the shrimp industry are eligible to receive reimbursement payments for expenses incurred during the dumping. Under the Continued Dumping and Subsidy Offset Act passed by Congress in 2000, those harmed by the dumping of imported shrimp will receive the proceeds of the tariffs once all appeals have been heard. Those eligible to receive these benefits

Continued...

include all of those who joined in the suit and other shrimpers who sent letters of support for the suit as well as some others in related industries supporting the action. The largest beneficiaries of reimbursements are likely to be those involved in shrimp processing because their operations are the largest, followed by the shrimp fishermen themselves.

Communities across an eight-state area have been affected by the impact of imported shrimp on the U.S. market. One such community is Bayou La Batre, Alabama. Nearly 85 percent of the population of this small southern town of 2500 people has been dependent upon seafood for their livelihood for generations. But in the last ten years, Bayou La Batre has fallen on very hard times. Shrimp prices have fallen dramatically. As a result, fishermen have been forced to make sacrifices in many areas of their lives such as health care, the purchase of automobiles, and education for their children in order to try to preserve their jobs as fishermen. Many fishermen have been unable to survive.

The Southern Shrimp Alliance estimates that one-half of all the boats of shrimp fishermen in the region have been repossessed. The *Mobile Register* reported that according to an insurance industry spokesman, most of the boats confiscated belonged to Asian Americans. In Bayou La Batre, 28 percent of the population are immigrants from Vietnam, Cambodia, and Laos. Following the Vietnam War, Catholic Relief Services resettled these immigrants in the community. According to Myra Sutton, longtime resident and United Methodist Woman, the Vietnamese "fought with our boys" in Vietnam. They served as guerrillas for the government. They brought the skill of fishing for shrimp with them when they were resettled in the United States, and they perhaps benefited from the guaranteed loan program that the U.S. government had at that time for the purchase of shrimp boats. In Bayou La Batre 3800 fishermen produce shrimp valued at some $30 million per year.[20] ■

Globalization Times

HANOI, December 2004 — "We believe that the decision to impose dumping tariffs on Vietnam shrimp imports into the U.S. is unjust and does not reflect the reality of shrimp production and exports in Vietnam. The decision is contrary to the principle of free and fair trade."

—Vietnamese government spokesperson[21]

"We shrimpers who work very hard on our shrimp farms are fortunate… Our shrimp meets the highest requirements for export to the United States. We do not get any subsidy from the Government in shrimp farming."

—October 12, 2004,
Letter of Vietnamese Shrimp Farmers to
U.S. Department of Commerce[22]

Continued...

49

The Vietnamese government expressed strong disagreement with the decision by the U.S. Department of Commerce to uphold the suit instituted by the Southern Shrimp Alliance. It maintained that Vietnam was not guilty of dumping and explained its volume of export of shrimp could be sold at lower prices because of favorable farming conditions, technology, and cheap labor. The head of Vietnam's largest shrimp exporter said that the tariff rates would affect profits, "...but the Vietnamese shrimp farmers and American consumers will be hurt most."

Shrimp is Vietnam's fourth-largest income earner. Aid agencies estimate that 3.5 million people in Vietnam are involved in the shrimp farming industry. On behalf of this larger number, in October of 2004, 2500 Vietnamese shrimpers sent a letter to Washington. The letter stated that:

"the preliminary decision of the Department of Commerce has caused a very negative impact and serious injury to our shrimp raising and trading. We shrimpers who work very hard on our shrimp farms are fortunate to have a favorable climate, employment and technological conditions for shrimp raising that produces high-quality shrimp."[23]

The Vietnamese shrimp are not caught in the wild but are grown on shrimp farms. The United States Agency for International Development (USAID), a branch of the U.S. State Department, and other international intergovernmental aid agencies such as the World Bank, as well as private nonprofit organizations like Action Aid of the UK have for several years been promoting shrimp farming in Vietnam as a poverty alleviation strategy. Action Aid contends that the effect of the tariffs could be to send many of these 3.5 million people back into poverty. According to the ruling, it is the small producers who will bear the largest tariff burdens. Action Aid prepared a report based on a survey of shrimp farming and shrimp farmers. The report explained that in some parts of the country fish farming was introduced because the rice fields had been made unfit for cultivation by the use of the defoliant Agent Orange during the Vietnam War. It is this development assistance to shrimp farmers that is considered an unfair subsidy under the rules of the World Trade Organization. Ironically, the reimbursements that will be available to those in the U.S. shrimp industry as a result of the decision about dumping are also considered subsidies by the WTO and therefore a violation of the trade rules. To date the U.S. Congress has refused to accept the WTO view.

Vietnam and other countries have threatened to take their case to the WTO in hopes that they will be able to impose retaliatory duties on U.S. products, notably soybean meal, the main food for farmed shrimp. ■

Please take a moment to make some notes about what you think is happening in these two situations and how you think the two are interconnected. How is economic globalization affecting people in both the United States and Vietnam? Who are the players, and what stake do the players have in the outcome? How are we involved? Use the Globalization Interconnections worksheet on p. 51 to make notes about the players.

see instructions on p. 50

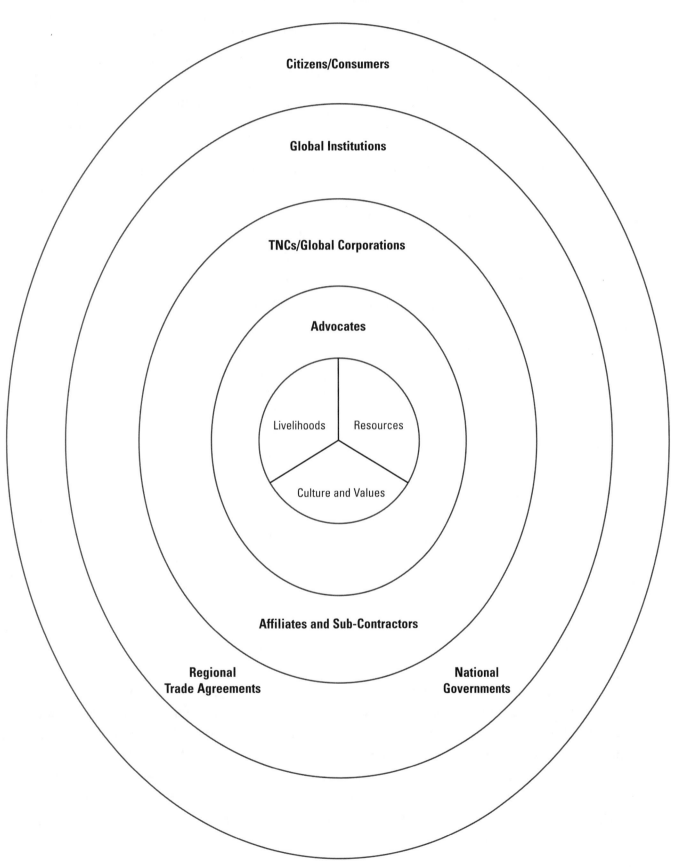

Citizens/Consumers

Global Institutions

TNCs/Global Corporations

Advocates

Livelihoods | Resources

Culture and Values

Affiliates and Sub-Contractors

**Regional
Trade Agreements**

**National
Governments**

What's Happening

These two situations present the competition between farm-raised shrimp and fresh-caught shrimp. These are very different processes—one is highly labor intensive, at least in the case of the Vietnamese, and the other not nearly so. Farm-raised shrimp is controversial because of the environmental impact of waste materials that are created in the process of the development of the shrimp. On the other hand, in the case of fresh-caught shrimp there are issues about the kind of nets used in order to protect sea turtles and other sea life. So the product itself, the amount that can be produced, the ways it is produced, and the impact of production are also a part of the reality of free trade.

What is happening has an impact on communities and affects how they experience change. In Bayou La Batre and other communities throughout the south where shrimping is the mainstay, immigrants from Southeast Asia are seeking to build a new life in a new country using an old skill. They face a continuing uphill struggle to be accepted in a new place. Immigrants and migrant fishermen are also involved in the production of shrimp. On the other side of the world communities are seeking to recover from the devastation of war, using shrimp farming as the means for pulling themselves out of poverty.

In the circle on the chart surrounding those directly involved in the industry are the corporations, those involved in importing and exporting shrimp, and in the U.S the organization CITAC (the Consuming Industries Trade Action Coalition) that takes a position in direct opposition to the Southern Shrimp Alliance. CITAC's interests span the two countries and the organization plays a key role in the setting of prices. It too has a stake in the outcome of the trade suit. The governments of both the United States and Vietnam are involved. In the United States at least three different governmental departments are involved:

1. The Department of Commerce, through its quasi-legal arm, the International Trade Commission, whose job it is to investigate trade-related interest injuries to U.S. industry;

2. The Department of Homeland Security that houses the Customs Department responsible for collecting tariffs and for determining who will receive the reimbursement payments;

3. The Department of State, charged with the responsibility of administering the development assistance programs of the U.S. government.

At the international level there are other aid-related agencies like the intergovernmental World Bank and Action Aid, a nonprofit secular private agency involved in development assistance. The work of Action Aid is not unlike many of the assistance programs sponsored by the General Board of Global Ministries, United Methodist Committee On Relief (UMCOR), and the Women's Division. Finally, there is the World Trade Organization, whose stake in the outcome of the suit is related to its responsibility for the management and oversight of compliance with the rules for global trade.

Ordinary citizens as consumers of shrimp products also have a stake in how the suit is settled. Shrimp is the most popular restaurant seafood in the United States. One way or another the outcome will affect the price we pay in the restaurant or in the supermarket. If we are citizens of the United States, the three United States departments involved in this dispute over free trade are technically all acting on our behalf. So whatever they do we are implicated.

Vulnerable livelihoods are at stake in the United States and in Vietnam. Free trade is about competition and as the experiences of the residents of Bayou La Batre and of the Vietnamese peasants demonstrate, competition can be a painful thing. For communities in both places livelihoods seem very precarious. In the case of the shrimp industry in the United States, the livelihoods of some 70,000 people are connected and at stake. In the case of Vietnam it is the livelihoods of those 3.5 million people choosing shrimp farming as a way out of poverty. Fluctuations in the price of shrimp in either place can have a devastating effect.

So it is not surprising that there is a considerable variety of perspectives on just exactly what free trade is. A spokesperson for the Southern Shrimp Alliance declares:

> Everybody bought into this idea of free trade. There are rules about subsidies; there are rules about trade barriers. Everyone agreed that all must abide by the rules. We like free trade—it means that there are certain rules and that there is no government intervention. The WTO has the job of making sure that each country obeys those rules. Each country has similar rules.[24]

Another commentator critical of the actions of the Southern Shrimp Alliance explained free trade this way:

> The shrimping industry is a great example of how the fight for free trade isn't about protecting big business at all. Rather, it's about protecting free markets, promoting commerce, and generating prosperity. It's about consumers having access to the best goods at the best prices, and employees and employers finding one another where they may— and doing both without deference or interference from artificial borders, protective special interests, or messy, over-arching governing bodies.[25]

In contrast there is the perspective from Action Aid Vietnam, the Vietnam fishery association, and the Vietnam farmers union:

> Such trade protectionism imposed by developed countries, particularly the U.S.A., not only violates the fair trade policies and practices but more seriously, it threatens the rights to food and livelihoods of millions of poor people that depend on production and trade of products that are traded internationally.[26]

And so the definition of free trade is a matter of perspective.

Livelihoods: Basics

Before beginning a full discussion of economic globalization and livelihoods, it is important to review some of the basic realities about the institutions and policies of globalization that were spelled out in the two preceding examples.

What is the theory of free trade?

- Each nation makes what it can produce most efficiently in comparison to other nations— this is called comparative advantage.

- Each nation sells or exports those things to other nations.

- Each nation buys what others produce most efficiently.

- There are no trade barriers (tariffs) or other rules to stop the free flow of goods.

What are the advantages of such a system?

- Consumers enjoy lower prices because efficient production means producers can deliver goods and services at a lower cost.

- Producers also enjoy lower prices because they can get cheaper materials for production.

- Consumers have access to more product choices.

What has been the experience of free trade?

- Low wages, low labor, and lower environmental standards are the comparative advantage for poor nations and poor communities.

- Free trade in money (investment) has increased speculation and helped to make some people very rich, while at the same time destabilizing entire economies.

- The possibility of mobile production weakens workers' bargaining power and threatens layoffs, pitting workers, often women, against one another in competition for the lowest wages (the so-called race to the bottom).

- Sweatshop labor makes possible lower prices for consumers and higher profits for transnational corporations and higher salaries for CEOs.

- Rich nations continue subsidies on certain products (agricultural subsidies that mainly benefit agribusiness, e.g., by 350-900%) while poor countries must cut subsidies in order to access international loans and markets.

The examples of Bayou La Batre and Vietnam make it clear that free trade has a major impact on workers in the shrimp industry. The chart below gives a more complete picture of the way in which free trade flourishes through the competition that pits worker against worker. The chart gives examples of four different kinds of workers from the U.S. context, describing their relationship to free trade. These examples are mirrored in the experiences of many types of workers in many countries around the world. You might want to add

---

WHAT IS A FREE TRADE AGREEMENT ANYWAY?

An agreement signed between two or more countries to:

- Remove "trade barriers," which are national laws, regulations, policies, or programs. Things like environmental standards or subsidies.

- Limit the power of governments to regulate private business.

- Promote the "free market" as the basis for all decisions.

Source: Polaris Institute, www.polarisinstitute.org

WHAT DO "FREE" TRADE AGREEMENTS COVER?

- Investment

- Products—agricultural and manufactured

- Intellectual Property Rights

- Services

Source: Polaris Institute, www.polarisinstitute.org

other workers who are also affected by free trade, such as agricultural workers or factory workers whose jobs have been eliminated as their factories moved to other parts of the world. Think about workers in your own community who clearly seem to be placed in a situation of competition with workers in other parts of the world. The chart below illustrates this race to the bottom and its effect of lowering wages for workers everywhere. The impact is greatest on the most vulnerable groups of workers, among them women (see chart on p. 56).

The World Trade Organization

The World Trade Organization (WTO) is an international financial institution with membership from more than 140 countries. It is responsible for developing and administering rules or treaties about trade. The roots of the

---

FREE TRADE AND LABOR:
WHO WINS IN THE RACE TO THE BOTTOM?

Day Laborers and Temporary Workers
In order to stay competitive, employers have turned to day and temporary employees. Temporary workers increased by 530% between 1982 and 1997.

"Informal Economy" Workers
Workers who can't find a place in the economy turn to individual entrepreneurship, legal or illegal, to make ends meet. Also, women are contracted to work at home, paid per piece for assembling and packaging for large companies, for example, utensil packages used on airlines.

Prison Labor
The rise of privately run prisons has also meant the use of prison labor—a way to cut costs by corporations.

Maquiladora Workers
In developing countries, free trade agreements bolster export processing zones where foreign companies are given tax breaks, etc. Factories often employ young women at the lowest wages. Factories move at will from place to place in search of the cheapest labor.

Adapted from *Economics Education: Building A Movement For Global Economic Justice*, Praxis/Economic Justice Project, American Friends Service Committee, 2001.

WOMEN AND FREE TRADE

The exploitation of women's work is key to free trade agreements and the neoliberal strategies that are part of the new global economy. Developing countries use their "competitive edge" to participate in the global economy. This means cheap and efficient labor, which is often women's labor.

Free trade profoundly shapes women's daily lives by:

- determining the cost and quality of the food they buy to feed their families;
- limiting access to public services;
- stunting the ability to find a good job that is safe and provides benefits;
- damaging the environment, affecting the overall quality of life and health of women;

- exploiting women's circumstances through export zone factories, using women's need for a job to subject them to low wages, no benefits, sweatshop conditions, and sometimes even forced birth control;
- forcing many young women in developing countries to work instead of going to school;
- contributing to the spread of HIV/AIDS because of women's need to leave their families to find work (they may return home infected with the virus);
- contributing to the erosion of subsistence farming and domestic agriculture in favor of export production, profoundly affecting the lives of the 50 to 75 percent of women of the developing world who are involved in agriculture.

Adapted from *Economics Education: Building A Movement For Global Economic Justice*, Praxis/Economic Justice Project, American Friends Service Committee, 2001.
Source: *Economics Education*, Praxis Project

WTO go back to 1944 when the General Agreement on Tariffs and Trade (GATT) came into being (the International Monetary Fund and the World Bank were founded in the same year). The General Agreement on Tariffs and Trade, which dealt only with trade in goods and had no legally binding power, became the World Trade Organization in January 1995.

Unlike its predecessor organization, the WTO's rules are legally binding. Often called the Supreme Court of international trade, the WTO has the ability to undermine the laws of sovereign nations. Decision making at the World Trade Organization is on the basis of one country, one vote. However, the most powerful countries—the U.S., the European Union, and Japan—dominate the decision-making process, often negotiating in secret, using aid and loans as leverage for compliance. The WTO acts as an arbiter of international trade disputes, but labor and environmental stan-

dards can be challenged as trade barriers under this system. Member countries are bound by its laws, making the laws that they pass in their own countries effectively meaningless.

The WTO rules are powerful tools for controlling the behavior of workers, nations, and governments. Review each of the rules in the chart "WTO/GATS Power Tools" on pp. 57-58 (keeping in mind the examples from the shrimp industry) and think about who benefits and who loses money in the exercise of these rules. Note the use of phrases like "irreversible access" and "equal treatment." Try to imagine the differences between countries rich and poor and in between.

- What might be the meaning of "irreversible access" to a poor country for its exports but also for its imports?
- What would be the difference in the meaning of "equal treatment" for small producers and for transnational corporations?

The power tools that advance corporate globalization currently in place and under negotiations within the WTO promote the interests of investors and big business. They also undermine local democracies, jobs, worker and human rights, common security, the environment and food safety.

The power tools unpacked:

Market Access Rule: This rule guarantees irreversible access to the markets of other member countries. Once a country agrees to provide market access for a particular service sector, foreign service providers must be granted unrestricted, irreversible entry into the country. Foreign shops can set up as many operations as they want, even if the increase causes economic, environmental or social change.

Most Favoured Nation Rule: Essentially grants sovereignty to corporate service providers from all other member countries by ensuring that host governments provide them better than equal treatment, regardless of their track records on social, labour or environmental issues. This applies to all services and can prevent any country or regional government from restricting foreign operators into their country using human rights, labour or environmental standards as a criterion.

Domestic Regulation Rule: Member countries must prove to trade tribunals that their regulations on technical standards, licensing, and qualifications are not "unnecessary barriers to trade in services" and "are not more burdensome than necessary." This rule leans heavily in favour of corporate interests and discourages governments from passing and enforcing environmental, labour and public health regulations. Local laws may be ruled illegal under the GATS.

Expansion Rule: The GATS agreement is designed for ever-increasing expansion. Member countries commit to successive negotiations to expand the agreement and increase the number and type of services that will be included. Like a ratchet it will constrain future governments' ability to exercise democratic and regulatory authority.

National Treatment Rule: This rule forbids governments from favouring their domestic sectors over foreign-based companies. Governments are prevented from supporting the growth of local providers. Right now, the national treatment rule applies to certain services in the GATS but the goal is to apply it across the board to all services including social programs.

Security Exemption Rule: The WTO bolsters military spending, weapons production and the international weapons trade. Through the security exception governments are exempted from WTO rules governing the trade in goods and materials it considers necessary to protect its "essential security interests." This rule permits subsidies to the aerospace and military-industry sectors and encourages traffic in arms, ammunition and implements of war.

Continued...

Penalty Rule: Countries cannot make modifications to the commitments they have made within the first three years and countries must negotiate "compensatory adjustments." This means a country will have to agree to compensate all other member countries who require compensation. Expect big business shops and lobby groups to press their countries to demand compensation—big time!

Dispute Settlement Rule: Disagreements between member countries about trade rules are resolved by tribunals composed of unelected trade experts who meet in closed sessions. They have the power to enforce their rulings by allowing the winning country to impose economic sanctions on the losing country until it changes its laws. These tribunals can rule against national, state, or local regulations that strive to protect the environment or public health simply by finding them "more burdensome than necessary."

Source: Polaris Institute, www.polarisinstitute.org

What's the Problem?

Perhaps the thing that stands out most clearly in the two stories just presented is the way in which free trade has created a situation that pits one worker against another. Each country tries to produce the product that gives it the best advantage. The United States and Vietnam are not nations equal in economic power so when their fishermen compete for a share of the market they bring different resources to the competition. Each of the two countries had a different perception of the meaning of "fairness." In a world of unequal power between nations it is difficult to imagine how appeals for the creation of a "level playing field" can meet the satisfaction of all.

Who are the beneficiaries of the competition between peasant shrimpers in Vietnam and modest income shrimpers in the United States? It would seem that the regime of free trade does not decrease the vulnerability of either group. The situation of the shrimp producers is one example of a kind of direct competition.

Small Farmers and Agribusiness

Another example of livelihood is the competition between U.S. farmers and farmers in other parts of the world, more precisely the competition between peasant farmers, U.S. family farmers, and U.S. corporate agriculture. The production of corn is a case in point. In Mexico and throughout much of Central America corn is a staple part of the ordinary diet. Corn is at the heart of both the Mexican culture and the Mexican diet. Three million Mexican farmers grow corn, as farmers in Mexico have been doing for centuries.

The United States government has a program of subsidies for its corn farmers, the majority of which go to large-scale corporate farmers. These subsidies make it possible for U.S. farmers to grow a surplus of corn that they can now sell on the Mexican market. Under the NAFTA agreement, U.S.-grown corn is able to enter the Mexican market at a price well below the price for which the Mexican farmer can afford to produce it. From the Mexican point of view this is dumping. The result is that thousands of Mexican farmers are being forced out of farming and off their traditional lands. If they can no longer farm they have two options: one is to go to the Mexican cities, particularly those near the U.S. border; the other is to cross the border into the United States looking for work.

The reality is that thousands of Mexican farmers have simply lost the battle to compete. Their adversary is not small farmers like themselves but large-scale agriculture subsidized by the U.S. taxpayer.

> "U.S. corn is grown on a massive scale on huge mechanized farms, keeping production costs—and prices—low."
>
> "The imports are squeezing out small producers. In less than a decade, subsidized corn has begun to displace communities who have successfully cultivated corn for thousands of years."
>
> —Make Trade Fair: Corn in the USA

Countries have different capacities to produce the same product. For the United States, part of that capacity is the ability of the U.S. Treasury to provide subsidies to those who grow corn. It is hard to see how trade alone can resolve inequalities between countries. Where is the balancing mechanism in the free trade strategy? Large-scale agriculture has the competitive advantage in the production of corn, but what should be the fate of Mexico's three million farmers and all of the family members that depend upon the work of those farmers? What about communities impacted by the large influx of immigrants who have left the land? Should Mexico have to depend on producers in another country for its most basic food, if it can produce that food itself?

Small Farmers and Consumers

Another example of the problem of competition between workers that touches us directly is coffee production. Markets in Europe and North America provide coffee for a large portion of the world's coffee drinkers. A number of countries in the developing world produce coffee, for example, Brazil, Kenya, Costa Rica, and many others. These countries must compete for a share of the market in developed countries. In the 1970s when there was trouble with the coffee crop in Brazil, Kenya had record sales and prosperity.

At the other end the coffee chain, we as consumers have some responsibility for the inequalities that are produced. As in the case of shrimp, in coffee production there are many actors in the journey between the coffee farmer and our coffee cup. The chart "From Seed to Cup," below, shows who will benefit most from the trading of coffee. The producers' share is the smallest of all—in fact, small-scale coffee producers are all fighting over six cents." How is it possible to imagine that earning that six cents can produce a sustainable livelihood, building a life of value, especially if others in the chain are receiving 64 cents out of every dollar?

FROM SEED TO CUP: FAIR SHARES OF THE PRICE OF A CUP?

Role	Share
Farmers (25 million families)	2%
Exporters	3%
Shippers	6%
Roasters (Nestlé, Kraft, etc.)	64%
Retailers	25%

Source: www.maketradefair.com

Outsourcing and Offshoring

Many of us who in recent years have lived in communities and watched factories close and relocate in other parts of the United States or the world know the pain that is associated with this reality, often just referred to as plant closings. There is also the experience of the threat of plant closings in which one set of workers is threatened by a company's ability to move the factory to another place and employ a different set of workers. The workers' control over their situation becomes greatly diminished. They have little bargaining power on terms for health insurance, pensions, and work rules. So the price of retaining the factory may be lower wages or weaker benefits.

Two corporate practices often implemented by transnational corporations escalate the idea of competition between workers:

Outsourcing occurs when a company or corporation takes one aspect of its production or service and transfers responsibility for that part of the work to another location. It might be another community in the same state or in a different state. But more and more companies shift aspects of production not just to places in the United States but to other parts of the world.

Offshoring is a term coined to refer particularly to transferring aspects of production outside the home base country of the corporation. Offshoring, according to the Congressional Research Service study refers to the "...practice among companies located in the United States of contracting out the performance of service sector activities (e.g., call center operations) to businesses located beyond U.S. borders." They add that the assumption was "...that the work sent overseas was being or could have been performed by U.S. workers."[27]

During the 2004 U.S. presidential election the issue of the offshoring of jobs became a major point of disagreement between the two candidates. Stories about the loss of U.S. jobs began to appear with great frequency in the press and the level of public anxiety rose dramatically. The reality is that very limited statistical information is kept on the subject, so most of what is known is by way of stories and press reports. In the box on p. 61 are some of the basic facts of this situation.

Migration

A companion phenomenon to outsourcing and offshoring is the migration and immigration of workers from poor communities and nations to more prosperous places in search of better economic conditions and opportunities. The chart on p. 62 tells that story.

OFFSHORING—SOME BASIC FACTS

How many workers are affected?

- Between 2000 and 2004, 4 percent of all layoffs among U.S. workers are attributed to offshoring.
- Job losses are only 3 to 10 percent of total jobs.
- Blue collar jobs are those most affected and still the most endangered.
- Fourteen million jobs are potentially outsourceable.
- It is estimated that 3.4 million U.S. workers (2 percent of one year's employment levels) will be affected by offshoring by 2015.

Why is Outsourcing Possible?

- Widespread dissemination of low cost, good quality technologies capable of high speed transmission of voice and data communications enable white collar offshoring.
- Expansion of technology skills and highly educated personnel with computer facility in English in countries of the Third World dramatically expanded the highly skilled labor pool.
- Responding to the recession of 2001, companies used technology to lower costs and to increase efficiency.
- Companies can realize cost savings between 45 and 59 percent through offshoring.
- Who is outsourcing? It is estimated that about 40 percent of Fortune 1000 firms have already outsourced some work.

Where Are the Jobs?

- Countries with abundant supplies of well-educated persons and of IT (information technology) and accounting skills, including China, Eastern Europe, India (185,000 jobs for a population of more than one billion) and the Philippines, become suppliers of white collar services to U.S. businesses and consumers.
- IT services can also be provided by a number of low-wage nations such as Argentina, Brazil, China, the Czech Republic, Hungary, Jordan, Lithuania, Mexico, Slovenia, Russia, and the Ukraine.
- China is the second biggest receiver of outsourcing service work by offering the lowest wages and an official ban on basic union rights.
- Mexico has lost several hundred thousand service jobs gained under NAFTA in flight to China.

What Kind of Jobs?

- Simple service work: processing credit card receipts, writing software codes.
- Processing home loan mortgage applicants, interpreting CT scans for hospital patients, preparing corporate financial analysis for investors, developing computer-generated printouts for industrial plants and residential housing, and many more.

Who Benefits?

- Indian workers earn one dollar or less per hour to handle customer service calls for firms like EarthLink and Travelocity.
- Indian computer programmers earn one-tenth of the pay of their U.S. counterparts to write code for multinational corporations like Citigroup.
- Supporters of offshoring contend that it lowers the cost of services for U.S. consumers and enhances the overall competitiveness of U.S. companies.

Government Responses

- Proposals have been made to use government-determined policies to assist businesses potentially affected by offshoring. WTO rules on government procurement banned the U.S. government from favoring U.S. firms in procurement contracts.
- The U.S. Trade Adjustment Assistance program offers displaced workers additional income beyond unemployment benefits as well as job training.
- The Worker Adjustment and Retraining Notification Act requires employers to give workers 60 days notice in writing of any closings or layoffs. Proposals are being made to ensure that these provisions will cover losses resulting from offshoring.
- Dislocated worker programs also could provide assistance to workers affected by offshoring.[28]

GLOBALIZATION AND MIGRATION

How Many Are There?

- 140 to 175 migrants worldwide

- 1 in every 35 persons is an international migrant

- 30 million people are migrants within their own country

Where Do They Come From and Where Do They Go?

- High Migrant Receiving Countries: European Union, United States, Canada, Russia, Australia

- High Migrant Sending Countries: India, Mexico, countries of Eastern Europe

Migrants in the Labor Force

- United States: 22 million workers representing 16 percent of all workers

- Germany: 4 million workers representing 10 percent of all workers

- Australia: 2.5 million workers representing 26 percent of all workers

Sending Money Home (2001)

- All Migrants: $111 billion per year

- Developing Country Migrants: $60 billion per year (equal to more than all the development assistance received)

- India: $10 billion

- Mexico: $10 billion

- Philippines: $6 billion

Sources: BBC News Global Migration Factfile; New Internationalist; BRIDGE, A Popular Education Resource for Immigrant and Refugee Community Organizers.

What is the Connection?

We have seen several different ways in which globalization creates competition between workers and farmers in different countries; between workers in rich countries and workers in poor countries; between middle-income workers in rich countries and middle-income workers in poor countries. As globalization reaches into every level of society there is rising public concern over this competition. In the past the United States has always boasted of its workforce as a part of its comparative advantage, especially its highly educated and highly paid workforce. But the new realities of globalization mean even a highly educated workforce is no longer insulated from the possibility of job insecurity. That promise of job security was a part of the American dream.

- What are the implications of insecurity about a job as a computer programmer with an income of $60,000 to $95,000 a year?

- Will these experiences of globalization force people in the U.S. to have a different view of themselves and a different attitude about the role of the U.S. in the world?

- What does it mean to the United States to be an importer of services when historically we have always been an exporter of services?

- What does it mean for those who are citizens of the United States to acknowledge that there are others in the world who can do those services just as well?

It is said that offshoring produces middle-class jobs in India. It is a goal of the United States to encourage the development of the middle class in other countries. At the same time, some commentators who address this rising competition between workers point out that the very act of expanding the middle class in other countries will in the future erode U.S. living standards.

- Are we finding ourselves in a situation of contradiction?

- Is it necessary to choose between maintenance of U.S. living standards and improving the living standards of persons in the other parts of the world?

- What is the difference between: 1) a global economy operating on the basis of comparative advantage, and 2) a global community?

- If each worker or nation thinks only of self-interest and advantage how is it possible to build a global community?

The wage gap between computer programmers in India and computer programmers in the United States is one to ten. Computer programmers involved in offshoring in India also enjoy a very large wage gap between themselves and the multitude of the poor of India. Globalization is a phenomenon that creates such dramatic gaps. What does it mean to promote an economic system in which there is both inequality within countries and inequality between countries?

In this connection it's important to remember the role being played by the global actors in this situation. By working in accord with WTO rules, transnational corporations have the tools to operate directly in other countries as well as to seek partners in other countries, to create subsidiaries, or simply to outsource all of their work. But these strategies contribute to a reality that pits workers against each other. Many charge that in seeking ever lower labor costs, corporations have a lowering effect on labor costs everywhere.

The Role of Government

Competition between workers also brings to mind the role of government in the protection of workers in the case of job losses over which they have no control. Up to the present time, the U.S. government has used a series of different kinds of compensatory measures: unemployment insurance, extension of unemployment insurance, trade adjustment assistance, and retraining programs. The situation raises the larger question of what the government's role should be in providing a safety net for its workers. What programs or guarantees will ensure the livelihood of workers? What strategies will protect their right to a job and an adequate standard of living? What should be considered an adequate level of livelihood? If the jobs of those earning relatively high salaries are insecure then we might ask the question: Who are the least of these?

The lifestyles of those living in the United States can mean that economic insecurity, even from the point of view of a very high income, can be very frightening. Many analysts suggest that a majority of companies have no intention of ever offshoring portions of their business. Yet the danger continues to be real in the minds of workers at every income level. The options open to individuals and families for coping with livelihood insecurity are more or less the same around the world: cutting health-care spending, taking children out of school, increasing women's work, finding ways to cut back on amenities and sometimes even on essentials like food.

Livelihood and the Good Samaritan

Before we turn our attention to what can be done about the problem let's revisit the story of the Good Samaritan. Imagine that traveling down the road to Jericho is comparable to a trip down the globalization highway. We are on that road, but this time we are all the players.

- In the global arena, who is the neighbor? Is the neighbor the Samaritan, is the neighbor the wounded man, or are both the neighbor?

- What does it mean that Jesus chose, not one of the faithful, but the foreigner, the stranger, or enemy as the person who sets the example of faithfulness?

- What is the vision of community that this story gives us? How big is our own vision of community?

- Is there is a Samaritan on our globalization highway?

From the stories of the shrimpers, the farmers, and the outsourced workers, it would seem there are plenty of wounded persons. But perhaps the neighbor is also the one who passed by, even if that person was not acting very neighborly. Perhaps those who stand by and watch as peasant farmers drift back into poverty are also the neighbor. On the globalization highway we are often bystanders. It seems that the action is taking place and we are powerless to help. Perhaps those who passed by on the other side wanted to help but didn't know how. Livelihoods are vulnerable in many parts of the world; the injured seem to be everywhere.

- From the globalization highway, how can we be neighbors to all of those who are vulnerable, all of those who were robbed and left for dead?

- If those of us living in the United States feel economically vulnerable, we feel as if perhaps we are that person who is wounded. How would we reach out to help another who was also wounded?

- What does it mean to be a person of relative privilege during very insecure times?

On the other hand, perhaps those who are passing by on the other side are the WTO and the governments—those somehow indifferent to the cries of the vulnerable; certain that their rules are right; certain that it is the right course to pursue their own interests, to seek hospitable climates for investments and transnational corporations.

- Are we, in our role as the religious community, the innkeepers in the cities that are on the globalization highway?

- Is the work of the United Methodist Church Office on Relief the work of the innkeeper?

- Is the mission giving of the Women's Division and United Methodist Women taking the role of the innkeeper, binding up the wounds, following the lead of others in mission, as well as striking out ourselves?

- And how does the wounded person have human dignity affirmed?

Think of the actions of the Good Samaritan binding up the wounds, using some of his own resources to arrange for caregiving. We don't hear the voice of the wounded person in the story. We don't know the person's reaction to this act of care, but we know that the Good Samaritan did some things himself. He himself put medicine on the wounds, he didn't simply turn the entire task over to someone else.

- Was the Good Samaritan then building community responsibility for the wounded man?

- On the globalization highway, how do we build community responsibility for the wounded persons of our world?

- On the globalization highway, who does our information reveal are the robbers?

- Remembering the basic facts in the story of the shrimpers, who are the robbers?

- Are free trade policies robbing persons and communities of the possibility of livelihood?

- In the story shrimpers in each place accused the other of robbery and of leaving someone for dead. If free trade policies are the robbers and free trade policies are being enacted on our behalf, are the robbers our own agents?

What Can Be Done and Who Will Do It?

"The indivisibility of human rights under-scores the understanding that freedom is hollow without food, that justice without jobs is like a clanging cymbal, and that liberty is a sham when people do not have land to inhabit and farm."
—General Conference Resolution 309. "Globalization and Its Impact on Human Dignity and Human Rights," *The Book of Resolutions, 2004*

One writer on globalization has suggested that what it is needed is a complete change in the outlook of both the U.S. public and its politicians toward this nation's role in the world:

Just as Americans are less secure when much of the world is plagued by extreme poverty, inequality and instability, worker exploitation overseas translates into exploited workers and less secure jobs at home. The electoral debate over outsourcing offers an opportunity to create a new policy approach that combines solidarity with self-interest in a whole-scale effort to benefit the entire world.[29]

What must we do in order to build the possibility of a sustainable livelihood for all?

NEGOTIATING THE GLOBAL COMMONS: LIVELIHOODS

- **Jobs**

- **Working Conditions—health and safety**

- **Health care, Child care**

- **Farmers and food**

- **Intellectual property rights**
  - Culture
  - Indigenous knowledge
  - Biodiversity
  - Access to essential medicines

- **Democratic Control**

The threats to livelihoods come at many levels. It comes at the level of global policy like the policies being enacted by the World Trade Organi-zation and in the same policies embodied in regional and bilateral trade agreements. Look back at the rules of the WTO (pp. 57-58). What is the attitude that questions:

- Are these rules working to diminish vulnerability of livelihoods?

- Can we only imagine what kind of rules we need in order to guarantee livelihood?

- What is our perspective on a strategy of comparative advantage?

- If there are places where comparative advantage works and places where it is not working at all, is it perhaps time to think about modifying the rules?

- How can we as workers take responsibility for ourselves but also recognize our connection to others?

- What do we need to do to recognize that our own well-being cannot be at the expense of others?

- Is there a way to say no to that particular idea of competition?

- Does the idea of the wage gap between countries and within countries force us to look again at what is really required for a sustainable livelihood?

- Are there things we need to change about our own lives? about our own patterns of consumption? Do we need to remember that wise remark, "live simply so others may simply live"?

Thinking About Alternatives

Even if they are made at the global level and far away from the daily lives of ordinary people, the strategies of globalization have consequences in our neighborhood. It is interesting to think about an alternative vision in our own community. Taking leadership in the effort to create such an alternative vision have been low-income workers who have lost their jobs to plant closings. These workers were clear that they needed to open the dialogue with workers in Mexico and other countries who were now employed in the factories. One of the positive dimensions of globalization is the ability of ordinary people to speak across borders. Sometimes it can be face-to-face, other times they will need to use the communications technology. Opening up those cross-border conversations can make a difference.

Another way to be personally involved relates to pension fund investments that many of us have. This is one place where we can hold corporations responsible for their actions. The churches have long pioneered the work of corporate social responsibility. The Interfaith

Center on Corporate Responsibility (ICCR) has developed a set of guidelines for proper corporate behavior.[30] Advocacy groups have also been involved in important "cross-border" efforts concerning trade agreements and their consequences.

Fair Trade

One way to open conversation on these issues is the fair trade movement. The goal of the fair trade movement is to try to increase the shares of producers and others in the global production process. Those working to make trade fair propose to secure fair prices for farmers and for consumers.

The UMCOR Coffee Project

All of us are consumers. One way we can begin to deal with globalization is to pay attention to what we are buying and how and why and for whom it is produced. The UMCOR Coffee Project is an ongoing effort already supported by The United Methodist Church as well as many other denominations. The project is an innovative way to help people in need while enjoying fellowship and an excellent cup of coffee. As Christians we can address a consumer dilemma by buying coffee that is fairly traded. United Methodist congregations that participate are helping small-scale farmers in Latin America, Africa, and Asia earn a fairer share of income, obtain access to credit and technical support, and gain a trading partner they can trust through a fair trade organization called Equal Exchange. This cooperative markets coffee produced by producer cooperatives and is involved throughout the chain of production helping to make prices fair for all.

In your congregation, a women's group, youth group, mission, or peace and justice committee might sponsor the UMCOR Coffee Project. Then as your congregation enjoys this high quality coffee, learn more about its impact on the people who grow it. Read about coffee farmers and the ways in which the church is helping people like them. Discuss issues of justice in the global marketplace and take action in the spirit of love. United Methodist churches have sustained UMCOR's ministries of relief and development for more than sixty years. With such commitment, we can also make a difference in this new way. Chocolates and hot cocoa and other products are also available.

Make Trade Fair

Oxfam, the UK-headquartered development assistance agency, operates the comprehensive web-based program Make Trade Fair. The project combines specific information about the free trade of a wide variety of products from coffee and corn to flowers and chocolate. The website includes specific advocacy strategies for work on each of the commodities as well as information of overall general interest in the right to food and fairness for farmers and other producers.

Ecumenical Week of Trade Action

The idea for an ecumenical week of action on trade began in November 2003 when over 100 trade activists from 50 countries came together in a conference. The aim of the week is to challenge the free trade myth, to put forward the alternative of trade justice, and to tell the other side of the free trade story. Activities around the world during the week are designed to put pressure on governments, particularly those of the wealthiest countries, and on the International Monetary Fund, the World Bank, regional and bilateral trade agreements, the World Trade Organization, and transnational corporations.

An action guide helps local groups think

about the issue and how to organize activities during the week, as well as including stories about the effect of trade on people's lives. A worship guide includes valuable resources for how to think about trade in a faith and liturgical context.

Cross-Border Dialogue

The Alliance for Responsible Trade (ART) a national network of labor, family farm, religious, women's, environmental, development, and research organizations, pioneered cross-border cooperation on trade advocacy in the early 1990s with its work on the North American Free Trade Agreement (NAFTA). It promotes equitable and sustainable trade and development. In March 2005, in concert with its partners Common Frontiers from Canada and the Mexican Free Trade Action Network,

ART issued a statement on the future of NAFTA on the occasion of a meeting between President George W. Bush and Mexican President Vincente Fox. The networks agreed that ending poverty and dealing with inequalities between the three countries should be at the top of the list for working on human security. They urged that measures be taken to protect and improve the environment and guarantee universal access to health services for citizens in all three countries. They affirmed that food sovereignty was a key issue for all three countries. All of these issues, they believe, have worsened under NAFTA. Finally, they urged the presidents to consider NAFTA a failed model and to listen to the growing number of voices speaking on behalf of an alternative vision for NAFTA and for the proposed Free Trade for the Americas agreement.

Sign of Hope: La Mujer Obrera Celebrates 25 Years of Struggle Against Globalization and Free Trade

El Paso, Texas, 2005

In 1981 a small group of primarily Mexican American immigrant women who were struggling to make a living in the garment industry decided that they needed to come together, to create a workers' center. The purpose of the center was to provide a place where they could strategize about how to improve their working conditions but also deal with all the other problems that they faced, such as poor housing, inadequate child care, lack of health care, inadequate legal knowledge, and protection. From the beginning, the women of La Mujer Obrera had a clear understanding of the concept of livelihoods.

The proposals for a North American Free Trade Agreement were a death knell for gar-

ment factories in El Paso. The women of La Mujer Obrera were among the first local groups who protested the potential impact of NAFTA on their jobs and livelihoods. They established links with their sisters on the other side of the border to work together on behalf of fairness for all workers. Receiving some assistance from interested organizations like the Women's Division, they were able to continue their work even as more and more workers lost their jobs. During the height of the struggle against NAFTA the women of La Mujer organized marches and demonstrations on both sides of the border to dramatize the need for a joint struggle.

Twenty-five years after its founding, La Mujer Obrera is continuing its pioneering

Continued...

efforts linking jobs, livelihoods, and advocacy for economic and social justice. With most of its members permanently displaced by NAFTA, the organization has asked the question, "In the midst of globalization, how do we, as women who are living the everyday consequences of underdevelopment, defend our rights and build sustainable communities rooted in justice and human dignity?" (From "La Mujer Obrera Year End Report," June 30, 2005, Southern Funding Collaborative, Special Initiative to Promote Capacity Building.)

Their answer has been a two-pronged strategy. Part one was the creation of the Center for Bilingual Development and Social Enterprise. The mission of the Center is to embed community organizing and leadership development in community economic development. There are three parts to the work of the center: (1) the Women's Institute, which provides training and critical analysis skills for Mexican immigrant women to build capacity to participate in the defense of their rights; (2) the Social Enterprise Center, which assists women to establish, operate, and grow businesses and micro-enterprises (known as social enterprises) that utilize their own cultural heritage in market-based strategies for achieving economic justice; (3) Community Development Initiatives that include five social purpose businesses and a museum and cultural plaza, which will promote the dignity of Mexican immigrant women and showcase Mexican culture.

Faced with the failure of NAFTA adjustment assistance to create a viable economic future for them, the women of La Mujer Obrera are using this initiative to create this future for themselves. In concert with this effort, La Mujer Obrera launched a campaign entitled "Break the Chains of Economic Violence," which included press conferences, meetings, and teach-ins to share information on the dev-astating impact of NAFTA on women workers and their families.

The second part of their strategy is the convening of the Women and Social Enterprise Network. "The Network is composed of women and women's organizations in the U.S., Mexico and Canada with experience in working at the intersection of economic justice and community economic development with and for low income women. The Network's goal is to contribute to the growth of the national/international movement for justice for low-wage workers in the midst of globalization." (From the Grant Proposal for Women and Social Enterprise Network, March 1, 2005.)

The 30 organizations of the Network are seeking to build effective enterprises that create real economic alternatives for low-wage women workers as well as act as a catalyst for broader change within neighborhoods and simultaneously develop women's skills, both as business leaders and as leaders in the social justice movement. The Network, which held its first gathering in Montreal, Canada, in September 2004, includes a wide variety of women's organizations, including African American child care workers from Philadelphia; Caucasian rural women from New Hampshire; and grassroots women's organizations from Oaxaca, Mexico.

Collectively the Network will research and synthesize recommendations for public policy and institutional change; build alliance with organizations and institutions (in both the government and the private sector), and advocate for policies and resources to support grassroots and national efforts. Finally, a key component of the efforts will be developing methods of evaluation that help the organizations determine how social change has been achieved through their strategy of "using capitalism to transform capitalism's ills."

Bayou La Batre Postscript

August 2005 — The largest crowd in a decade was on hand for the fifty-sixth annual blessing of the fleet at Bayou La Batre harbor. New developments may dramatically alter the future of the shrimping community. A prominent developer and former candidate for governor is proposing a $200 million makeover of the community. The revitalized Bayou would become part of an area-wide effort to capitalize on the tourist potential of the Intra-Coastal Waterway area of south Alabama. Condominiums, spas, and tourist and retail shops may replace currently unused waterfront and city-owned dock properties. In another nearby area condos under development sold for $400,000 to $800,000.[31]

Reactions to the plans for the new developments are mixed. According to a report in the *Mobile Register*, a prominent ship owner said the plan "…could change the future of the Bayou dramatically but it won't be anything but castles in the air if property values skyrocket suddenly as rumors and news of the project spread."[32]

One shrimper who sold one of his two boats last year was more optimistic and said he welcomed the prospective development: "A lot of folks have problems with condos and such, but I'd rather see (the city) go that way than go vacant."[33] A more pessimistic view speculated that the well-attended fleet blessing might be the final blessing for Bayou La Batre because the development will shut down the seafood industry and "Bayou La Batre will be nothing more than a mud hole."[34]

October 2005 — But Hurricane Katrina has placed a very dark cloud over even these new prospects. *The Tampa Tribune* reported that two weeks after the hurricane the Gulf of Mexico was polluted and off limits to shrimping. In addition, all the major processing plants were destroyed. Many boats and lives were lost as some shrimpers chose to stay aboard their boats in an effort to save them. Joey Rodriguez, Bayou La Batre shrimper and boat builder, summed the situation up this way: "It's the straw that broke the camel's back for some of them. If you're somebody who was already down to the last thread of survival, just keeping the bills paid, this will leave you flat out."[35]

Chapter 4 Global Media, Information, and Communications Technologies

Christians, as citizens, have an obligation to exert whatever influence they can to ensure that the mass media in our society operate to serve the public good rather than merely commercial interests or those of individuals.

—"Global Communication for Justice,"
A National Council of Churches Policy Statement, November 1993

Whether we live in urban, suburban, or rural areas of the United States, global media and information and communications technologies (ICTs) touch our lives. The technologies of cable and satellite TV, cellular phones, ATM machines, and the Internet have become a familiar part of daily living. Global media enabled by these communications technologies that perhaps we don't understand but enjoy, have an increasing though sometimes hidden influence on our lives. These media communicate what is going on in distant parts of the world, informing us about who and what is fashionable.

The realities described in earlier chapters, such as the instant movement of money between countries for investment purposes and global assembly lines, have been made possible by these very same technologies. Now more than ever, information and knowledge are products to be bought and sold as well as to be used to generate wealth for individuals and corporations. We are reminded of how advertisers make use of the media to get us to buy a particular product. In some ways it is we ourselves as consumers who are being sold by advertisers; we are the "commodity" that corporations want to capture. Hand in hand with the transformation of information into a commodity has been the consolidation of control over media. Since the 1980s, the government's own pursuit of strategies to loosen control on media ownership through deregulation has moved the process along.

Information technologies are not neutral; they convey values: "…technologies often carry a built-in ideology which is so deeply embedded that one can't have a technological transplant without getting at the same time an ideological transplant—the biases and values and mindsets carried by the technology," ventured E. F. Schumacher, author of *Small is Beautiful*. What we see and hear through the media, as well as what the media chooses not to show us, can make a difference in our understanding of reality. As the same corporations take ownership of both news and entertainment, the distinction between the two is blurring. This means that those who control what we see and hear are very powerful.

Communications technologies make possible instant communication across great distances. We were there via television at the taking of Baghdad. Does the use of these technologies begin to make us feel that the only acceptable communication is one that is instant? Are we impatient with any news that takes more than thirty seconds to tell? Digital technologies also make possible the perfect reproduction of artistic forms of communication like music and movies at a nominal cost to the producer, so that beyond the initial investment everything else is pure profit. We have come to accept these megaprofits as their due.

It is important to think about the right to communicate and how it is affected by the present ownership structure of global media and information technologies. We need to look at the structure of control of global media and information technologies and examine the messages:

• Are the forces of global media building a global community, and if so, a global community of what sort?

• How do our desires as consumers shape the messages, or are the owners of that media shaping our desires?

• What happens to values of justice and equity in this new age of information?

• How do we meet our responsibility as Christians to exert influence to ensure that mass media and communications serve the public good?

"The Global Consumer" (see centerfold, pp. 84-85) presents a humorous way of thinking about how our images of ourselves and the way we live can be shaped by media advertising.

> Take a few moments to think about your own life and its interconnection with technologies like ATM machines and cable or satellite TV. Make a list of some of the technologies that you use frequently.
> You may be surprised at how deeply you are involved with information and communications technologies.

Globalization Times

BANGKOK, THAILAND — The thirty-one-year-old journalist Supinya Klangnarong and four editor co-defendants are facing civil and criminal libel charges, including damages of up to $10 million (for which Supinya would have to work 2777 years in order to earn enough money to pay the company). She suggested publicly that the Thai media conglomerate Shin Corporation benefited directly from government policies instituted by the Thai prime minister, Thaksin Shinawatra, who was the founder and former head of the corporation. The government's telecommunications policy changes gave maximum benefits to telecommunications companies and may cause possible loss of government revenue and, increasingly, unfair business services for the public. The corporation charged that Supinya's comments resulted in losses in credibility and business opportunity.

Supinya, who is General Secretary of a small non-governmental organization, the Campaign for Popular Media Reform, gathered information as a part of her academic

Continued...

research. The research results showed a four-fold growth in profits for the Shin Corporation ($980 million) between 2001 (when Prime Minister Thaksin's political party came to power) and 2003. The legal issue is whether it was against the law for Supinya to publicly express a view about conflict of interest on the part of the Prime Minister. But for Supinya, it goes beyond the issue of free speech:

> The major issue is whether the advancement of telecommunications technology will really guarantee the universal improvement of humankind's well-being or the rights of access to information; the rights to have alternative choices or the freedom of expression for every sector of society... The majority of Thai citizens are still mired in poverty (in the period from 1990 to 2001, 32.5 percent of the Thai population lived on two dollars a day[36]) and deprived of basic rights in communications—either access to information, technology, and freedom of expression.[37]

In spite of government telecommunications promotions policies, Supinya found that there is a lower level of utilization of telecommunications resources for public services in education, health care, and cultural, social, and democratic development. The major beneficiaries of Thailand's expanding communications industry are private concerns rather than the public and public services.

During the 1990s, Thailand experienced rapid economic growth as one of the "Asian tigers" through the institution of aggressive market oriented policies. It was, however, hard hit by the Asian financial crisis of 1997 when key economies in Asia (Thailand, Indonesia, and Korea) collapsed as a result of the precipitous withdrawal of investment funds by Western investors, with devastating effects on ordinary citizens.

The Shin Corporation is an example of conglomerate media ownership. Its mobile phone company, Advanced Information Services, was ranked among the 1000 Most Valuable Companies by *Business Week* magazine in 2004, and is made up of twenty-four separate companies operating across a spectrum of services: telecommunications, media, computer, satellite, and ICT technologies. These include the only provider of satellite communications services, Ipstar, which in 2004 concluded an agreement to provide broadband services for Australia and New Zealand as a part of plans to tap into the market for high-speed Internet services across the Asia-Pacific region. The corporation owns a controlling interest in Thailand's only independent television station as well as a number of radio stations. The corporation also controls Thai Air Asia, a budget air carrier which competes with the government's Thai Airways.

Prime Minister Thaksin has been compared to Italian media mogul, and Prime Minister, Silvio Berlusconi because he is a billionaire and reputed to be the wealthiest person in the country. The Prime Minister founded Shin Corporation in 1983 but stepped down from his post when he became the Prime Minister. He contends that media should not criticize government, because government would be hurt around the world, damaging the country and causing its foreign investments in the region to suffer.

Social justice and human rights activists around the world have rallied to support Supinya and to highlight the connections between an aggressive free market economic recovery strategy and freedom of the press in Thailand. The World Association of Christian Communications (WACC) that represents 900 communications institutions and communications professionals in 90 countries provided a scholarship for Supinya's journalism studies. "Shin Corp.'s decision to pursue the case

Continued...

against Supinya has serious implications not only for her personally, but for Thailand's standing in the community of nations," wrote the WACC president and general secretary in a letter to the Corporation. They continued that the case is against Thailand's Constitution, "as it aims to punish the defendant for simply voicing an opinion on the relationship between the Corporation and the current Thai government."[38]

Human Rights Watch Asia Division warned that the suit against Supinya and her colleagues threatened to stifle press freedom in Thailand: "When business mixes with politics at the highest level in Thailand, it's impossible to distinguish a libel suit from an attempt to silence the Prime Minister's critics."

When asked why she was singled out for legal action when her views had been both held and voiced by others, Suypinya said: "Maybe because I am a symbol and I am young, a woman, and how dare I talk to you [Shin Corp.]? It is not common in Thai society."[39] ■

Globalization Times

OAKLAND, CALIFORNIA — "When stuff goes down in our communities, young folks are listening to KMEL, not watching the news. If it doesn't get air on KMEL, we don't know it's happening."
—Oakland Youth Organizer

In 2001, youth organizers in Oakland and San Francisco were frustrated by the fact that although there had been dramatic decreases in juvenile crime, nationwide, news coverage of crime had increased 83 percent. Particularly frustrating was the fact that on KMEL, the local hip-hop and R & B station that principally serves an audience made up of youth and people of color in the Bay Area and is owned by the media conglomerate corporation Clear Channel, images of youth as gangsters and criminals predominated. Further frustration stemmed from the fact that the station chose to fire its community affairs director Davey D., who, in the view of youth organizers, had shown interest in community concerns.

Community-based organizations working on a variety of issues—criminal justice, economic justice, and educational justice as well as groups representing local artists and the Community Youth Media Council—formed the Community Coalition for Media Accountability. They decided to initiate their own study to monitor KMEL program content, hiring homeless youth and activist youth as researchers.

The 2002 report of the Youth Media Council, *Is KMEL The People's Station? A Community Assessment of 106.1 KMEL*, charged that the station was failing to live up to its claim of being the "people's station." One of the key programs monitored was a public service program known as Street Soldiers that was promoted as addressing important youth issues in the community but focused on individual responsibility rather than the social conditions that lead to community problems. Media Justice Advocate for the Youth Media Council (YMC), Taishi Duchicela, gives more detail about the period in which the study was made: "It was a time when violence was decreasing in Oakland, but the radio station's coverage of violence was increasing. There were no youth voices, there were no organizing groups that were working on this, present on the radio airwaves."[40]
Continued...

The YMC study's major findings included the following:

1. KMEL content excluded voices of youth organizers and local artists.
2. It neglected to discuss the policy debates affecting youth and people of color.
3. It focused disproportionately on crime and violence.
4. It had no clear avenue for listeners to hold the station accountable.[41]

In contrast, during the same period, The National Association of Broadcasters recognized KMEL for outstanding community service: "KMEL has invested more time, money and manpower towards Bay area communities by teaming up with local organizations throughout the cities of San Francisco and Oakland." The Clear Channel website (www.clearchannel.com) highlights numerous activities of their stations with local charities such as the American Heart Association and local food drives.

KMEL's parent company Clear Channel has acquired a total of 1200 radio stations in the United States since the 1996 Telecommunications Act removed the cap on station ownership, and it operates in 65 countries worldwide. Clear Channel's range of companies includes radio, television, outdoor advertising, and live entertainment venues that sold 30 million tickets in 2003. Its revenues in 2004 were $9.4 billion. Their website identifies the following as one of its corporate goals: "We believe the ultimate measure of our success is to provide a superior value to our stockholders."

The Youth Media Council sees connections between the ownership of the station by Clear Channel and the policies of community relationships and content that it pursues. On the one hand, Clear Channel asserts that all stations are locally owned and are totally responsible for the content of their programming. Clear Channel Radio has ten million listeners each week. The corporation asserts that Clear Channel Radio does not operate according to any political agenda or ideology, and that local management makes programming and community events decisions based on their understanding of their audience interests and extensive audience research. "The Corporation values 'local spirit'; Clear Channel people and properties show their local spirit in countless ways in every community we serve."[42] A number of stations have co-sponsored "support the troops" activities, but the corporation insists that this is local initiative rather than corporate policy directive.

Youth Media Council monitoring presented another perspective. YMC discovered that KMEL programming consistently portrayed youth as gangsters and failures, solely responsible for the problems they face, and focused on youth violence. There was no discussion about the institutions that are involved in the creation of violence in the community. There was no mention of racism as a root cause. The Council believes that stereotypes portrayed in the media influence public policy. They contend that if those images are negative then there will be a negative effect in the community. Youth Media Council Media Justice Advocate, Taishi Duchicela, gave an example: "There was a ballot proposal which was called Measure FF, which would bring a hundred more police into the Oakland streets. The theory: more police means more protection and therefore less violence. Policies like Measure FF influence the conditions that we live in; they affect our lives. Measure FF would directly affect youth in our community. That's why we say media is a life-and-death issue because people get their information from the news, and people make policies based on the media."[43]

Youth Media Council also believes that media represents both a threat and an opportunity. A threat because images portrayed in the media can negatively affect the lives of their constituency—youth and people of color. At the same time it represents an opportunity to get their voices heard. "It is a forum to get

Continued...

general social justice for everybody. Imagine TV if it were really good, what real information we could receive. That opportunity is for social justice because if we had real media that would be covering stories about youth, we would be talking about that there are community organizations out there working on youth issues," Duchicela said.[44]

For the Council, ownership of media is a key issue. It notes that the 1996 telecommunications Act cleared the way for corporations like Clear Channel to acquire an unlimited number of radio stations, and therefore to be in a position to exert great influence across the country.

KMEL response to the Council's first report was limited. They produced a 90-minute edition of Street Soldiers called "360 Degrees of Violence." In that program, youth from organizations working with youth and on issues of violence were allowed to talk about youth violence in their own way, in their own words, in their own voices.

The Council plans to use the mechanism of broadcast license renewal to continue its struggle to build community accountability at KMEL. Once every eight years the Federal Communications Commission reviews the licenses granted to radio and television stations. (See Appendix, p. 147 for a description of FCC responsibilities.) California radio stations will be reviewed in 2006. The review process includes collection by the station of a public file of letters of comments and complaints.

These letters have to be kept on file, and they are reviewed by the FCC at the time of license renewal. The YMC campaign, called "For the Love of Radio UNPLUG CLEAR CHANNEL," will urge the public to submit letters of their views to KMEL's public file. The Youth Media Council Broadcast License Campaign will target KMEL and a Bay area talk radio station that is also owned by Clear Channel. The Council's goal is to create an infrastructure of community accountability that will mean that the station with the listenership of more than 600,000 people, 50 percent of whom are youth and people of color, would come closer to living up to its boasts of being "the people's station." The specific goal is to increase relevant local content on both KMEL and KNEW (Clear Channel's right-wing talk station in the Bay area); to increase media accountability and control, including the reinstatement of the position of community affairs director, and revocation of the Clear Channel licenses for the two stations. The YMC Media Justice Advocate concluded: "The community has to own media at all points…because we are the media right now, we are the content for the media. That means from policy to content to ownership of infrastructure to program work. In order to have media justice we need to own these points of production. We need to have complete control and power in order for us to be telling our own stories, or our stories to be heard, or for our community to really exist."[45] ■

Before we begin to think about the similarities between the two stories from Thailand and California, take a minute to jot down some of your initial reactions to these two stories.

• Are there winners and losers in the stories?

• Does the action of corporations in the stories seem to echo anything that we have learned about the action of corporations in the other stories so far?

• Do the problems of freedom of speech and community accountability seem very far from your own reality?

• Why do you think it might be important for us to understand global media when we are thinking about globalization?

What's Happening?

From Thailand we can see that one corporation exerts extensive control over access to a wide range of media communications possibilities—cellular phones, television, radio, Internet service. We see that the ownership of the infrastructure is critical to what media can do. Roberto Verzola, an environmental activist from the Philippines, has described the growth of consolidated control as the rise of a new landlord class that he names the "lords of cyberspace."[46] They are enriched and grow as they collect rents for services across the breadth of their corporation, ownership of both the content and the infrastructure of global media and communications.

Perhaps the most striking similarity in the two stories is the fact that both Supinya and her colleagues and the groups in the Youth Media Council are confronting corporate power. In each case the interests of citizens seem to be pitted against the interests and power of global corporations. Perhaps this helps to make the point that global corporations do not necessarily have local and national loyalties but rather loyalties to profits. Also, in both instances, people's organizations are struggling against globalization as a reality of consolidated or monopoly ownership. In Thailand, one company owns almost every dimension of communications. In the case of Clear Channel, the ownership pattern is not the same, but nonetheless it is comprehensive in the sphere of radio. Who are these corporate media actors? Just how much involvement do they have in our lives?

This insight leads us to another. The possibility of corporate consolidation of power in both cases seems to have been enabled and enhanced by the operation of government policy. As the monitor or gatekeeper for corporate access to "public" communications media, government can formulate policies that are designed to expand corporate ownership or restrict it. Shin Corporation's enhanced position would not have been possible without changes in Thai law. Similarly, Clear Channel could not own 1200 radio stations if the Telecommunications Act of 1996 and the Federal Communications Commission deregulation efforts had not removed the ownership cap of 28 stations, as well as permitting ownership across media sectors: radio, television, cable companies, and so forth. In Thailand and in the United States the stories point to the privatization of the "public" media. This makes it possible for the same company to control both the content of media and the technology and distribution system for bringing that content to the public.

The two stories raise the issue of the changing role of government in relationship to media:

- What are the definitions of terms like "independent media" and "free speech" in the context of globalized media?

- What are the responsibilities of media to be responsive to community perspectives, to be an independent eye and voice on local and national events?

- How close are the connections between governments and media giants?

- If media giants benefit from government policy, is it more likely that those media outlets will be supportive of those governments?

Operating in these two stories is the struggle to define the right to information and the right to communicate in the context of globalization and global media interests.

- What rights do communities of youth and people of color in Oakland have to expect information that represents their perspectives and that assists their community?

- What rights do Thai citizens have to learn about connections between their government officials and private corporations, and what right do they have to speak about these matters publicly?

- Do youth and people of color in Oakland have a right to communicate that includes some dimension of ownership of the media in their own community?

- Both stories assert that there should be some accountability between the people, media, and government. We see how identity as defined by age, race, and gender can influence who has access to communications technologies and resources. Can this be a dimension of what is called the digital divide?

> "By concentrating on the commercially successful strategy of serving 'mass tastes' in entertainment, the media have never adequately served the interests of the majority of people and seldom those of marginalized peoples. Neither have they served minority groups, neglecting to program for their cultural, racial, artistic and justice concerns."
>
> —"Global Communication for Justice," A Policy Statement Approved by the General Board of the National Council of the Churches of Christ in the USA, November 11, 1993

These two stories help us to think about a different kind of commodity, about information and culture as commodities. Information and culture are bought and sold in the marketplace. Whether the information is "news," culture, or music, it is treated no differently than shoes and cars in the age of economic globalization.

Globalization Interconnections

Using the Globalization Interconnections—Global Media Chart on p. 79, spend a few minutes thinking about the interconnections involved in global media. Under Resources in the center of the circle, consider some of the media and information technologies themselves: radio and newspapers as well as others, both the hardware and software that make global media possible (cellular phones, the Internet, fiber optic cable, and so forth). Under Livelihoods, enter some of the different kinds of technology jobs that affect your life, as well as those related to media. Finally, in the inner circle jot down some of the contents of that media message. What is being talked about? Whose point of view is being expressed? Whose culture and values are being demonstrated?

Moving outward, we can next list some of the justice advocates. Have you heard about any other groups that are interested in media justice? Some are mentioned in the stories.

Next we get to name the global media and information conglomerates. There are the corporations that create and own the hardware technologies of global communications, and the media corporations that produce the information software. Through a system of interconnected relationships they control virtually all commercial global media and communications. It is a vast interconnected network involving a multitude of companies, but dominated by a small number of megacorporations. List a few of them that you know.

National governments played important roles in our stories. In addition, in the United States, local and state governments were involved along with several federal agencies that administer laws and regulations, the Congress, and the President. Fill in any of those that you remember. Although they did

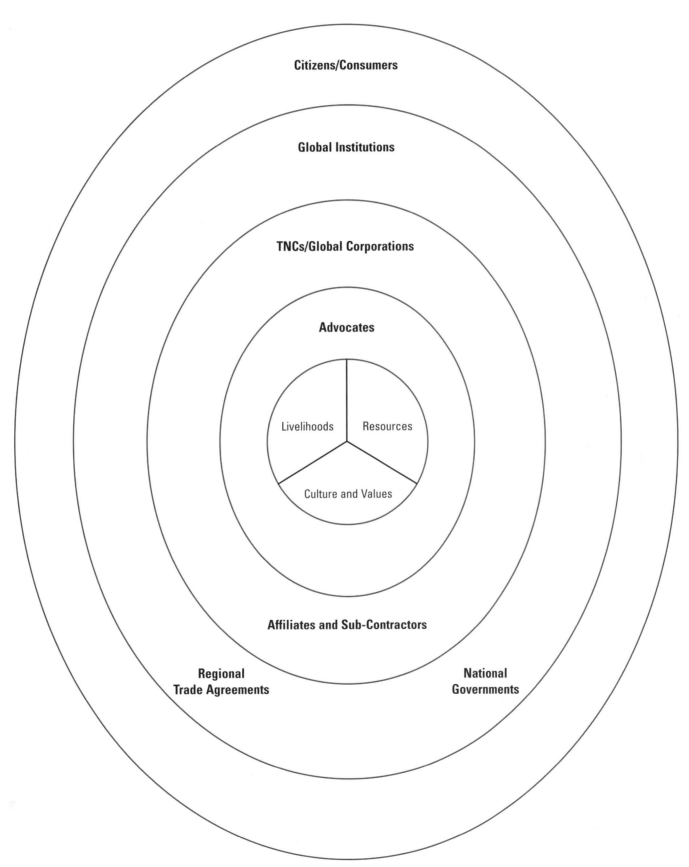

Citizens/Consumers

Global Institutions

TNCs/Global Corporations

Advocates

Livelihoods | Resources

Culture and Values

Affiliates and Sub-Contractors

Regional
Trade Agreements

National
Governments

not appear in the stories, later we will learn how the World Trade Organization and the World Intellectual Property Organization, the organization that with the WTO oversees all patents and copyrights, are deeply involved with global media and ICTs.

In the final circle we find ourselves again in our multiple identities: as citizens, as audiences and consumers of global media products, and as the product that is being sold. Our desires, needs, and appetites are sold by advertisers to various corporations and by media in order to enhance the wealth of the corporations. Note how these identities connect us to the other circles.

The Cyberlords

A cardinal principle of economic globalization is said to be that competition makes things work better for everyone, but an essential reality of media, communications, and information technologies in the age of globalization is the reality of concentrated ownership and consolidation. This reality gives a whole new definition to the classic understanding of competition and competitive advantage. It means that one company can have large holdings in one media sector the way Clear Channel does in radio, but it might also have holdings across several media sectors like the Shin Corporation does, or both simultaneously. This is why the title Cyberlords seems fitting to describe the operation of the sectors.

Names like Disney, AOL Time Warner, and Microsoft are familiar to most of us. But to understand what is happening and what is at stake in economic globalization's impact on media, communications, and information, we need to understand more about how this sector is organized. A good place to start is with some of the corporations whose products touch our lives every day—the media and entertainment industry. Ten megacorporations operating in many countries control much of the media that we see and hear every day. These ten corporations have revenues of some $416.6 billion each year. Some of these corporations have revenues that approach the size of those of some poor countries. Their media interests are varied. The chart Global Media Communication Conglomerates on p. 81 is a representation of the typical interconnections of global media business. Not all companies have all these connections but the majority have most of them.

Several of the megacorporations are also major book publishers. Television stations, cable networks, and cell phone service provision are part of the interconnected network of the cyberlords. The Disney Corporation is a case in point. Disney, which began with cartoons, is now operating a wide variety of related businesses: theme parks, magazines, theatrical productions, ABC television, the Disney Channel, online cable, and several other online ventures, as well as 720 Disney stores worldwide. When Disney makes a movie it can be shown in the theaters that Disney owns. If it's a children's movie, toys can be sold in stores that also belong to the company as well as through an exclusive franchise with McDonald's to sell Disney related products. Advertising for the movie can be featured in the magazines and newspapers and outdoor billboards that the company may own. The rights to its release on cable or television will be controlled by the company, so it will be shown on its own cable and TV networks. The righthand side of the Global Media Communication Conglomerates chart also shows that megamedia companies do not restrict themselves to media-related enterprises; they are also involved in a wide variety

GLOBAL MEDIA COMMUNICATION CONGLOMERATES

Print Media
- Books
- Magazines
- Newspapers

Music

Radio

Internet

Sports Teams & Facilities

Global Media Communication Conglomerates

Television
- Network
- Cable
- Satellite

Telephone Service
- Local
- Long Distance
- Cell

Movies

Theme Parks

Other

- Waste Treatment
- Water Management
- Gift stores
- Calling Cards

- Aircraft Engineering
- Credit Financing
- Bottled Water
- Heating

- Secretarial Services
- Greeting Cards
- Theatre Productions
- Mortgages
- Electronic Games

WHAT ARE THEY WORTH?

Corporation	Revenues ($ Billion)
General Electric	126.9
AT&T	66.6
Sony	53.8
Vivendi Universal	37.2
AOL Time Warner	36.2
Walt Disney	25.4
Viacom	20.0
Bertlesman	16.6
News Corp	11.6

of other activities from waste treatment and bottled water (as we saw in Chapter 2) to credit financing, mortgages, and aircraft engineering.

Another dimension of the reality of the cyberlords is the way in which competition operates among these large corporations. In their book *The Global Media: The Missionaries of Global Capitalism,* analysts Edward Herman and Robert McChesney describe three kinds of relationships these companies have with each other: "(1) on some occasions they are adversaries in competition with each other; (2) on other occasions they are prized customers for one another, selling or buying each other's products and services; and (3) on other occasions they are key partners combining for joint ventures." One of these corporations may own a small but substantial share of another. Liberty Media, a spinoff from AT&T, owns shares in AOL Time Warner, Viacom, and News Corporation. So these corporations interpret the globalization value of competition in a very special way.

Also connected to the megacorporations are supplier corporations that provide services for the megacorporations or serve as a conduit for their products. For example, Clear Channel's 1200 radio stations play music paid for by the record companies that are owned by the mega-media corporations and control and distribute music for most major artists. It is no wonder, then, that local artists like those that are a part of the Youth Media Council have difficulty getting airtime.

Of key importance in the interconnections with these large corporations are the corporations that produce the infrastructure hardware and software necessary for the operation of global media systems. So large corporations like Microsoft are also key players in the world of global media. As we shall discover later, there are some independent companies, but the patterns of ownership indicate that it is a very difficult world in which to try to be an independent.

If a single corporation or several large corporations control every possible source of access to a particular piece of information, what happens if for political or economic or cultural reasons they want to either withhold, distort, or embellish that piece of information?

The interlocking world of the cyberlords is portrayed on p. 83. Roberto Verzola suggests that this world embraces two kinds of production. The first is information, which is the software side. It includes a variety of things from information software for computers and databases to film and publishing. The second is industrial production, including the hardware of communications, from the Internet and integrated circuits to theaters, cable and radio production, and ownership. Ownership structures might be of both single and/or related production entities and ownership across several production types. The box with the dotted line in the center of the chart shows how the global media corporations just discussed are involved with both types of production.

The products and services offered touch not only media communications and entertainment, but as was noted in Chapters 2 and 3, information/communications technologies essential for financial transactions and payments. So in paying your bill online or by telephone you are participating in the world of the cyberlords.

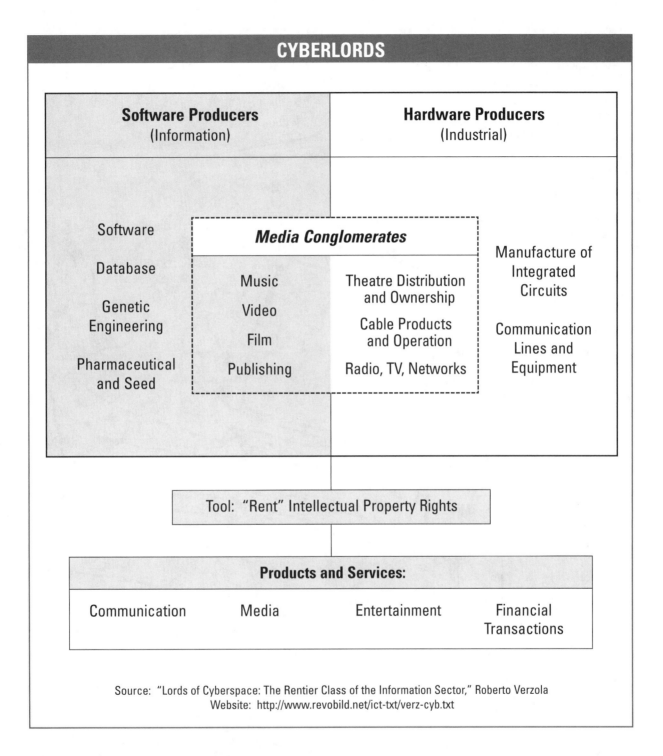

CYBERLORDS

Software Producers (Information)	**Hardware Producers** (Industrial)

Software

Database

Genetic Engineering

Pharmaceutical and Seed

Media Conglomerates

Music
Video
Film
Publishing

Theatre Distribution and Ownership

Cable Products and Operation

Radio, TV, Networks

Manufacture of Integrated Circuits

Communication Lines and Equipment

Tool: "Rent" Intellectual Property Rights

Products and Services:

Communication   Media   Entertainment   Financial Transactions

Source: "Lords of Cyberspace: The Rentier Class of the Information Sector," Roberto Verzola
Website: http://www.revobild.net/ict-txt/verz-cyb.txt

The work of the corporations across these broad sectors involves the employment of thousands of workers in the United States and around the world. The "Portrait of Women Workers in India" box (p. 86) gives a picture of women employed in the information technology industry in India that can be a counterpoint to the picture of Indian technology workers presented in Chapter 3. Take a moment to study the box and think about how this is another side, a women workers side, of big corporations and big profits.

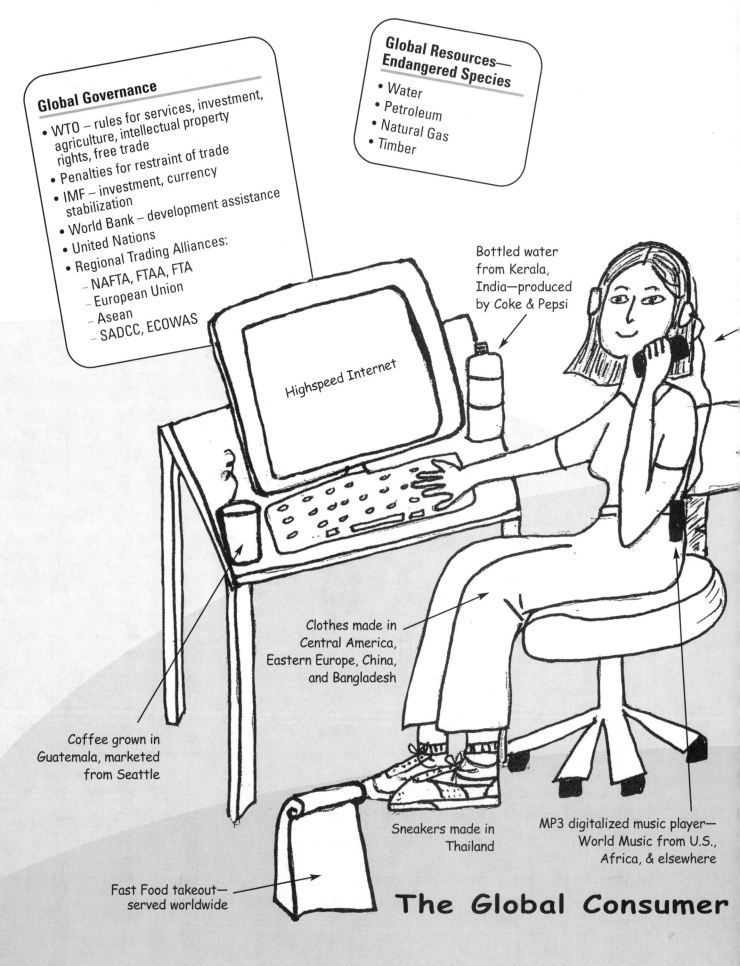

Global Governance

- WTO – rules for services, investment, agriculture, intellectual property rights, free trade
- Penalties for restraint of trade
- IMF – investment, currency stabilization
- World Bank – development assistance
- United Nations
- Regional Trading Alliances:
  - NAFTA, FTAA, FTA
  - European Union
  - Asean
  - SADCC, ECOWAS

Global Resources— Endangered Species

- Water
- Petroleum
- Natural Gas
- Timber

Bottled water from Kerala, India—produced by Coke & Pepsi

Highspeed Internet

Clothes made in Central America, Eastern Europe, China, and Bangladesh

Coffee grown in Guatemala, marketed from Seattle

Sneakers made in Thailand

MP3 digitalized music player— World Music from U.S., Africa, & elsewhere

Fast Food takeout— served worldwide

The Global Consumer

WHAT'S GLOBAL

Global "Culture"
- Shopping Malls
- MTV
- Internet – World Wide Web

Global Investment
- $1 trillion traded electronically each day
- Casino global economy – speculative investment
- Foreign direct investment – making things/making money
- National treatment of all corporations
- Big investors – insurance companies, banks, pension funds, mutual funds, 500 super-wealthy individuals

Cell Phone (operator based in Barbados or Bombay)

Japanese LED Monitor

The Global Consumer
- Cell phone
- Bottled water
- Computer
- Music video
- Designer clothes
- Starbucks coffee

Global Corporations
- Maximizing profits, minimizing costs
- No national accountability, national political and economic influence
- Instant communications
- Rights like an individual
- Make it quick, make it flexible, make it cheap

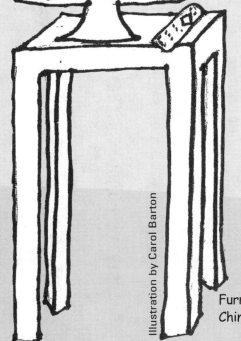

Illustration by Carol Barton

Furniture made in China, Sweden

Global Workforce
- Flexible and low wages
- High tech, white collar
- Women
- Migrants and immigrants
- Young
- Vulnerable

PORTRAIT OF WOMEN WORKERS IN INDIA

HOME-BASED WORKERS

Who: Married women with children, with basic marketable skills

Tasks:
- Medical and legal transcription
- Maintenance of daily accounts

Clients: Individuals and small businesses in Europe and North America

Compensation:
- Irregular pay
- Less than optimal wages

Liabilities:
- Computer purchase
- Electricity bills
- Internet connectivity costs

Terms:
- Informal contracts
- No easy legal remedies

CALL SERVICE CENTERS—DIGITAL SWEATSHOPS

Who: Middle class English-speaking girls

Tasks: Handling customer inquiries and complaints with patience and composure

Clients: U.S. customers

Compensation:
- Above average wages
- Air conditioned transportation to and from work
- Climate controlled workplace with piped music

Liabilities:
- No social life
- Working hours completely upside down to match U.S. time schedules
- Need to develop American accent
- Isolated from labor movement
- Potential for displacement by Chinese workers who will work for less
- Mind numbing and stressful work

Terms: 3 shifts:
- midnight to 8:00 a.m.
- 8:00 a.m. to 4:00 p.m.
- 4:00 p.m. to midnight

A common denominator of a large number of the products and services owned by the cyberlords is that they involve intellectual invention and creativity. We pay the cyberlords for the opportunity to listen to or use that creativity. That creativity is the corporation's "intellectual property." Maintaining control of that intellectual property is viewed as absolutely essential to the corporation to make and expand its profits.

Since the late nineteenth century, governments have taken steps to protect creative productions through a system of patents and copyrights. It is not surprising to discover that global media and information technology corporations have exercised considerable political influence to make sure that international intellectual property rights treaties remain in place and are strengthened. The system of intellectual property rights lets global media and information corporations control the market completely to their own advantage, limiting and controlling competition from others, because patents and copyrights can protect ownership rights and revenues for very long periods of time.

Intellectual Property Rights

In 1995, at the conclusion of the decade-long trade international negotiations that resulted in the creation of the WTO, one of the new items placed on the trade agenda was a consideration of intellectual property rights. Prior to 1995, intellectual property rights had been protected under a series of international agreements that were monitored by the World Intellectual Property Organization. With the creation of the WTO, a new agreement was established called the Agreement on Trade-Related Aspects of Intellectual Property Rights (TRIPS). The goal of the agreement was to establish a set of uni-form standards and practices for all countries on the issue of intellectual property. National legislation in developing countries had to be rewritten and expanded in all areas, including medicines, in order to conform to the new international agreed-upon standards. Before 1995 some developing countries, short of resources, simply ignored intellectual property rights laws and copied certain products, particularly movies and music, that had been under copyright or patents.

On p. 88 the main provisions of the TRIPS agreements are outlined, along with the kinds of products covered, the basic principles of the treaty, and the monitoring and enforcement bodies. Some of the basic principles referred to in Chapters 2 and 3 are included; that is, national treatment, in which equal treatment is given to local and foreign producers, and "most favored nation" treatment, in which equal treatment is given to all WTO members. The new agreement expanded these principles to the area of intellectual property. A new principle was added stating that it was important for the intellectual property rights regime to also make a contribution to technical innovation and to the transfer of technology. Although the agreement calls for benefit to both the producer and the users; and for economic and social welfare to be enhanced through the intellectual property rights protection system; there is often a conflict between the benefits to the corporate creator and to a society that will use the product. The situation is most dramatic in the case of medicines, such as drugs to treat HIV/AIDS and other diseases. A 50-year patent gives western pharmaceutical companies monopoly control over the quantity and price of these desperately needed drugs and was preventing poor countries from developing or purchasing generic alternatives from middle income

TRADE RELATED INTELLECTUAL PROPERTY RIGHTS (TRIPS) AGREEMENT, 1995

"Everyone has a right to the protection of the moral and material interests resulting from any scientific, literary, or artistic production of which he is the author."

—Universal Declaration of Human Rights, article 27.2

Countries covered: All members of the World Trade Organization

Protections

Patents including life forms, pharmaceuticals, and indigenous knowledge— 20 years	Trademarks	Geographic indicator names	Industrial Design— 10 years	Copyrights— literary, artistic, musical, photographic, audiovisual, computer programs— 50 years	Design of integrated circuits— 10 years	Trade secrets

Sectors Involved

Information technology	Agriculture—genetically engineered foods	e-commerce	Telecommunications

Basic Principles

- National treatment
- Most favored nation
- Contribution to technical innovation and transfer of technology

Doha Declaration 2001

- TRIPS Agreement should not prevent countries from taking measures to protect public health
- Exemptions for pharmaceutical patent protection in least developed countries until 2016

Monitoring and Enforcement

Global	• World Trade Organization • World Intellectual Property Organization
National	• Federal Communications Commission • National Telecommunications and Information Agency

develdeveloping countries. The right side of the TRIPS Agreement chart on p. 88 outlines a special declaration agreed to by the WTO in 2001, which was an attempt to get around this problem. However, a World Council of Churches study on globalization concluded that the terms of this arrangement were so complex that no government has been able to meet them.[47]

The impact of the current TRIPS Agreement can also be seen in the area of information and communications technologies. Computer programs are regarded as literary works under the TRIPS agreements. Since there is a 50-year intellectual property rights protection, any country seeking a transfer of computer program technology has no choice but to buy the technology and related products from the current copyright holders. U.S.-based corporations earned $38 billion in royalties from a variety of patents in 2000.[48] In 1998 the U.S. Congress extended the copyright for individuals to 70 years beyond the life of the author, and for works owned by corporations to 95 years. The developers of the technology are largely English speakers; similar new developments in alternative languages will be slowed by copyright protection. Is it any wonder, then, that English is the unofficial/standard language of the Internet? Imagine the potential revenue of a 50-year copyright to the megamedia and information corporations.

Intellectual property rights were created to honor and provide fair compensation for innovation and creativity, and they are named in the Universal Declaration of Human Rights. But in an age of economic globalization, they may serve as another tool to solidify corporate monopolies and to lock individuals, communities, and countries with limited resources out of the benefits of technological innovation. It is a process that builds on existing social and economic divisions, and is often spoken of as the digital divide.

The Digital Divide

Predictions on the impact of the digital divide are varied. The National Information and Telecommunications Agency report, *Falling Through the Net,* in 1999 gave evidence of a real gap between the technological haves and the technological have-nots. Public resources available to date have not alleviated the significant use gap between the rich and the poor.[49] By 2005 optimistic government studies from Europe suggested that divides were "transitory."[50] Only time will tell, but perspectives like those of former chairman of the Federal Communications Commission, Michael Powell, remain food for thought. This view suggests that those nations that are able to harness the power and opportunities that technology offers will rise to greatness, and those who do not will whither in every aspect—education, art, war, philosophy, and politics

If former FCC Chairman Powell is correct, in order to understand fully the effect of the principles of economic globalization on media communications and information, we need to think about who is moving ahead and who is falling behind. Much has been written about the possibilities that Internet technologies create—E-business, E-commerce, E-education, and so forth—all developments that are often touted as a sign of the success of economic globalization. There is no doubt that new opportunities are opening. One lesson from the experiences of the Youth Media Council might be to question not only who has access to these opportunities, but also whether these opportunities are taking people where they want to go.

If we accept that there have always been patterns of inequality in our nation and between nations, we can see how the impact of new information and communication technologies has been to further complicate those patterns of inequality, changing some for the better and some for the worse.

The "Digital Divides—Which Side Are You On?" chart (p. 91) presents ways to think about the digital divide. The left side of the chart presents U.S. Internet usage by gender, education, location, family income, and race. In the nation as a whole, Internet use is at 60 percent. The differences between men and women and urban and rural areas may seem surprisingly narrow. Predictable use differences exist based upon education and family income. Racial/ethnic differences show a wide range, with white and Asian/Pacific Islander groups above the national average and black and Latino groups lagging considerably behind. The statistics mask the disparities that may exist when viewed through the intersection of factors like race, family income, education, and gender.

The box on the right makes a comparison between the Internet use of people in high-income countries like the United States, Europe, and parts of Asia with the least developed countries in Asia, Africa, and Latin America. Usage in high-income countries is ten times, and in some cases one hundred times, greater.

It is important to keep in perspective the extremes that continue to exist in our world: 80 million people using the Internet every day as compared to 80 percent of the world's people who have never heard a dial tone. We may need to ponder whether the resources are available to bring information technologies to that 80 percent, and whether that would be the best use of those resources. Do the processes of globalization give societies the option to choose which information technologies to use and how to make them serve their own development needs?

> "Our priorities are hygiene, sanitation, safe drinking water. How is having access to the Internet going to change that?"
> —Supatra Koirala, who works at a private nursing home in Kathmandu, Nepal (BBC News Special Report: "Information Rich, Information Poor," 1999)

> "Media need not divide peoples and cultures. It can make it possible for persons, communities and nations to participate fully in their own cultures as well as in shared world meanings and values. Media can't enable people to participate in community and the national life."
> —"Policy Statement on Global Communications for Justice," National Council of Churches, November 1993

What is the Larger Problem?

Global media and information technologies—the message and the medium—can offer exciting new possibilities for building global community. But as we have seen from the stories of Supinya and Youth Media Council, the road ahead is not an easy one. The consolidation of ownership, the expanded pace of media deregulation, and other developments have occasioned a major crisis of values related to media and information technologies, a crisis that jeopardizes the realization of possibilities. In the present reality, economic globalization has contributed to a fundamental contradiction. This is the contradiction between media and communications as an instrument or tool in the public interest, and media as a vehicle for

THE DIGITAL DIVIDES – WHICH SIDE ARE YOU ON?

Digital Divide: The gaps between individuals, households, businesses, countries, and geographic areas at different socioeconomic levels with regard to both their opportunities to access information and communications technologies, and to the use of the Internet for a variety of activities.

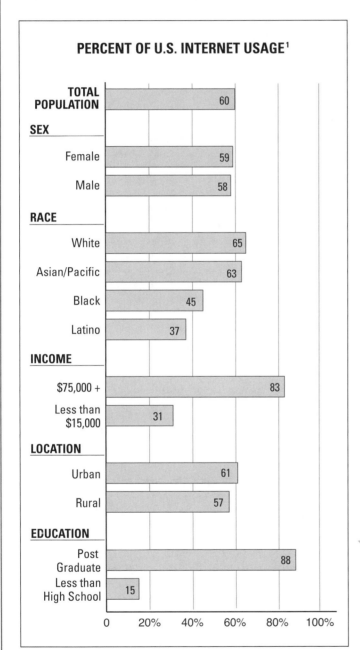

PERCENT OF U.S. INTERNET USAGE[1]

	Percent
TOTAL POPULATION	60
SEX	
Female	59
Male	58
RACE	
White	65
Asian/Pacific	63
Black	45
Latino	37
INCOME	
$75,000 +	83
Less than $15,000	31
LOCATION	
Urban	61
Rural	57
EDUCATION	
Post Graduate	88
Less than High School	15

UNITED METHODIST CONNECTIONS[2]

Total Churches	34,892
Total Districts	514
Total Annual Conferences	63
Churches with Website	6,864
Districts with Website	307
Annual Conferences with Website	63

All Boards and Agencies have websites.

GLOBAL INTERNET USERS[3]

World	9.9%
United States	55.0%
High Income Countries	45.5%
Developing Countries	4.9%
Latin America & Caribbean	8.1%
Sub-Saharan Africa	.69%
East Asian/Pacific	6.0%
South Asia	1.5%

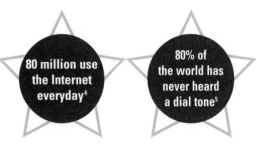

80 million use the Internet everyday[4]

80% of the world has never heard a dial tone[5]

SOURCES:

1 www.ntia.doc.gov/ntiahome/dn
2 InfoServ–UM Communications
3 "Recasting this net–information commons cash cow"

4 United Nations Human Development Report, 2004
5 BBC News, 1999

furthering a particular economic model that promotes a global consumer culture. Social goals like universal service—which posits that everyone should be able to have access to basic information—so long at the center of U.S. communications policy, are now being challenged by corporations who consider the value of the provision of universal service as restrictive regulation.

The Universal Declaration of Human Rights Article 19 addresses the issue of the rights to information:

> Everyone has the right to freedom of opinion and expression; this right includes freedom to hold opinions without interference and to seek, receive and impart information and ideas through any media and regardless of frontiers.

Take a few moments to think about the items included on the Negotiating the Global Commons: Communications worksheet (on p. 93) for media and ICTs. The sheet lists some of the following issues: monopoly control, commercialized media culture, public interest and voice, access/connectivity, uses, and resources.

- What are your views on these critical issues?
- What are the values that guide our thinking?
- Where do we imagine there will be differences of opinion in our communities?
- How can we use media and ICTs to build global community?

It might be helpful to use Article 19 of the Universal Declaration of Human Rights as a kind of yardstick to consider the issues. The article itself points to the capabilities necessary to fully realize the right to communicate.

Here are some questions that you might want to ask yourself in thinking about the Negotiating the Global Commons: Communications and ICTs:

- Who owns information and knowledge? Is it utilized for private benefit for a few or the public benefit of many?
- How is knowledge disseminated and distributed? Who are the gatekeepers? Where does knowledge that shapes your opinions come from? Who owns that source?
- What role might ICTs play in the eradication of poverty and the establishment of gender justice?
- What constrains and facilitates the use of knowledge by people to achieve their goals? Who is best and worst positioned to take advantage of this knowledge?

Information as Global Commons

Reflecting on growing public opposition to consolidation of media trends, FCC Commissioner Michael J. Copps said: "At stake…are our core values of localism, diversity, competition, and maintaining the multiplicity of voices and choices that undergird our marketplace of ideas and that sustain American democracy." [51]

Our contemplation of values will require that we think of information as global commons in a way that recognizes the interdependence of

NEGOTIATING THE GLOBAL COMMONS: COMMUNICATIONS

- **Monopoly control**

- **Commercialized media culture**

- **Public interest and voice**

- **Access/connectivity**

- **Uses and resources**

the messages of global information and media and the medium—the technologies themselves. Let's first think about some of the value questions that we will need to confront when thinking about the messages of global media and information technologies.

- How believable is knowledge that comes wrapped in a commercial package?

- Can we accept everything that claims to be knowledge that may perhaps be the message crafted by media owners for commercial or even political purposes?

- How important is the clarity of message to us and what means do we have for insuring that clarity?

- Does consolidation of the media mean that only the voices of the powerful few will be heard? Are we facing a loss of space for informed debate?

- The experiences of both Supinya and the Youth Media Council would suggest we have something to think about. But if we are sitting in our comfortable living rooms and comfortable communities, is it harder for us to recognize that we're listening to the voices of only the powerful few or recognize that some voices are missing?

- We can also see from the stories that there are very different capabilities of ensuring that we hear the multiplicity of messages. If we are hearing messages that reflect our own thinking, what responsibility do we have for making sure that the voices of others are heard?

- And how shall we deal with the global

commons of information technology? Information technologies can leapfrog development so that technologies like cellular phones can make it possible for some communities and nations to jump over the problem of needing resources to establish land lines. But what kind of priority should the creation of a cell phone infrastructure be, or an Internet connectivity system in communities or countries with limited resources?

Millennium Development Goals

In 2000, the nations of the world working in the United Nations created a series of development goals called the Millennium Development Goals (MDGs). One of those goals calls for the creation of an international structure of cooperation. A subgoal in that strategy is the provision of information technology infrastructure for developing countries. In general, the weakness of the goals is that there are no clear systems of accountability for how these goals will be achieved, and they rely heavily on the market to solve problems that it is in part responsible for creating. It seems completely appropriate that goals related to an international information communications technology should be linked completely to a system of international cooperation. But this goal also needs to be linked to the other goals that relate to alleviation of poverty, provision of safe drinking water, women's empowerment, and so forth. For us, the question of value will be whether or not we have a way to think about international information and communications technologies, not as ends in themselves, but as means or tools to use in the creation of global community—means that we as the Christian community could support and nurture.

In the United States we value the possibility of access to information as a part of our under-standing of equal opportunity. How do we begin to extend that value to include the means and resources that are necessary to expand the possibility of being connected to information and communications technologies, and then being trained how to use them? If information technologies are available in a community, but only on a commercial basis and requiring training to be able to use them, we can see how capabilities are involved. These other things represent the capabilities that are necessary to realize the right to information that access alone cannot accomplish.

The Good Samaritan and the Right to Communicate: Who is My Neighbor?

The road to Jericho is like the global information superhighway today, both a magic road that can take us to exciting places and a very dangerous place. Let's put ourselves inside the story of the Good Samaritan and see what lessons it might teach us about the right to communicate. On the information superhighway there clearly are robbers. Perhaps the robbers are those cyberlords, the conglomerates controlling all of media and communications technologies. They want to control our access to information technologies, and their control robs others of voice.

In the story of the Good Samaritan we never hear the voice of the person who has been robbed. We do not know that person's thoughts. He seems to have been robbed of the ability to tell his own story, to describe the nature of the injustices he has faced. He has been robbed of the right to communicate. On the information superhighway perhaps the victims of the robbery are persons from minority communities, or perhaps it's even ourselves. It would certainly include those persons living in poverty in the Third World, particularly in Africa, who have little possibility of access to global information technologies. All of those who are robbed are dependent upon someone else to tell their story, and often that someone else is the person of another race or nationality.

And just who are the passersby on this information superhighway? Perhaps they include those of us in the developed countries, together with the elite of the Third World, who are users of the information superhighway. We are worshipers of the Internet gods and secure in our own connectedness, but unaware and sometimes uncaring about whether others have been robbed of their voice.

But others who may be passersby are global communications companies themselves who look at the robbed person and find this is not a very interesting story to tell. After all, poverty and robbery are old news, and advertisers probably don't find it an interesting way to lure customers at all. From a corporate point of view, the robbed don't represent any market constituency that is big enough to influence corporate profits.

Who are the good Samaritans on the information superhighway? Perhaps they are workers for media justice like the Youth Media Council and Supinya or the whole host of other organizations that work at the national and international level on media and communications policy issues. Or perhaps they are those technology wizards that are creating alternative systems to share technology or to make available systems of community radio.

Also on the information superhighway there are the innkeepers, those who take the responsibility for mobilizing international support for the right to communicate. They include organizations like the World Association of Christian Communication that came to Supinya's aid in her battle against the Shin Corporation. These groups use the Internet, email, blogs, and a whole host of free information websites committed to creating and sharing the widest possible body of knowledge, redefining the concept of intellectual property rights to safeguard the right to communication for all. The innkeepers are also organizations like the Youth Media Council that build capacity within community organizations to produce and control their own media and information.

So who is my neighbor on the information superhighway? The medium itself makes the whole world our neighborhood.

> "The existing global web of communication—symbol, images and pictures simultaneously transmitted into scenarios and sequences of events—catch and hold the lives of people everywhere...The church is called to resist when any force subjugates the spirit, mind, will and voice of people to the dictates of any worldly power...Thus the church has a critical interest in media structures, control, audiences and effects."
> —"Policy Statement on Global Communication for Justice," National Council of Churches, 1993

What Can Be Done?—Restoring and Affirming the Right to Communicate

We have learned from Supinya and the Youth Media Council that in order to affirm and make real the right to communicate, we must understand the connection between the content of media and information and its ownership. The two stories have shown how local action can address both of these aspects of global media and information.

The global concentration of ownership of media can be seen in the ownership of media within our own communities, as well as in national networks and information systems. Perhaps in media more than in any other place, the reality of economic globalization's impact is felt most deeply and most completely. U.S. government policy on global media and information technology is like a sound that reverberates both close to us and far away. Justice action on global media and information will have to have the same reverberation. If U.S. policy can be changed from the local level through the state level to the national level within the United States, then it is possible to imagine that U.S. government strategies at places like the World Trade Organization and the World Intellectual Property Organization will have to be different. Voices other than, or at least in addition to, corporate media voices can also be heard.

In February 2005, United Methodist Women in the United States joined women and men from 102 countries for a day of monitoring of the news on TV, radio, and in newspapers. The project was called the Global Media Monitoring Project—Promoting Gender Equity in the News Media, and was coordinated by the World Association for Christian Communication Women's Programme. For many of those involved in the project around the world, monitoring was one way to gain very important information about how media is operating and what messages it is sending. The aim was to look at both the quantity and quality of the news. Women involved in the media-monitoring project were able to identify and analyze what was portrayed in their local community. This kind of media monitoring effort provides half of the kind of information that is needed. Once we have some information about the content of the media message it will be important to discover ways to learn about the patterns of ownership.

The Media Empowerment Project of the United Church of Christ

The Media Empowerment Project provides many useful tools to help groups get started thinking about the impact of media locally. The project has produced an organizing manual that provides "a resource for communities interested in organizing around media. It provides a framework for understanding why media matters and how different aspects of media are related; useful facts and statistics; stories of successful grassroots campaigns; and a chapter of resources on different tactics and skills for organizing around media." The manual provides information about both local cable services and Internet broadband and how to investigate local media.[52]

Local Action Opportunities

Local Access Cable

Two companies—AOL Time Warner and Comcast—dominate cable service throughout the United States. In exchange for their use of the local airways cable companies are legally required to provide communities with some sort of public service. As a part of their local franchise agreements cable companies must make a contribution to a pool to provide public access for individuals, governments, and educational institutions. This pool of resources can then be used by communities to televise government meetings and other local events. In this era of tight local budgets, the use of this pool of resources is now under much debate. Local governments, sometimes strapped for resources, must consider whether this money might not be better used to fill potholes or for other needed activities, rather than to be used for community cable service. Community cable service could provide an opportunity for concerned Christians to raise important issues like gender images in the media within local communities. Community cable service could provide an opportunity to create programming that would raise these and other important issues to local citizens; or a platform for voices that are otherwise unheard in local communities, like people living in poverty or immigrant communities. If this is to be possible, it is important that local cable access be preserved as a part of the means for achieving the right to communicate; that cable companies continue to be required to contribute to this pool of resources; and that local governments continue to affirm the importance of guaranteeing local capability to exercise the right to communicate.

hereusnow.org

A project of the Consumers Union, this is a website with extensive information on consumer communications issues. From its information on media ownership, local communities can discover who owns the media in their community as well as the kind of actions local communities around the country are taking. We can start working on global media justice in our own community.

Community Broadband Access

Local communities now have the possibility and capability to control and offer free or low-cost broadband Internet access. This possibility could be another important way to bridge the digital divide that exists within local communities. However, cable and telephone companies like Verizon want to have all broadband service privatized. The companies would then dictate the terms and have the right to refuse service. Communities across the country are not equally served by Internet connectivity; rural communities and low-income communities do not necessarily receive the same service as urban and high-income areas. Large corporations often pick only the most profitable areas to serve. How are underserved communities or those with limited ability to pay going to receive Internet service?

The 1996 Telecommunications Act established a policy initiative for broadband universal service. The goals of universal service are to: "promote the availability of services at just,

---

THE TELECOMMUNICATIONS ACT OF 1996

The promise:
- More competition, more jobs, more diversity, lower prices.

The provisions and consequences:
- Radio station ownership cap lifted— radio giants like Clear Channel created, substantial drop in minority-owned stations, homogenization of play lists, less local news.
- Expansion of limits on local TV station ownership raised to 35 percent of all viewers—increased media mergers and concentration, five companies control 75 percent of primetime viewing.
- Cable rates deregulated—rates increased by 50 percent between 1996 and 2003.
- Cable broadcast cross-ownership rules eased—90% of top cable stations and broadcast networks owned by the same networks.
- Digital cable license given to broadcasters—$70 billion of potential federal treasury revenue lost.
- Broadcast license term extended from five to eight years—broadcaster accountability to the public weakened.
- Universal service fund created— made funds available for community cable access.
- V-Chip requirements established—allows parents to control television programming for children.

reasonable and affordable rates; to increase access to advanced telecommunications services throughout the nation; and advance the availability of such services to all consumers including those in low income, rural, insular, and high cost areas at rates that are reasonable comparable to those charged in urban areas. The Act also mandates that all providers of telecommunications services contribute to a federal universal service fund."

A battle is now being waged in statehouses across the nation to prevent local communities from establishing their own broadband systems. Bills have been introduced in 15 states that would prevent cities from providing their citizens with Internet access. Five states have already passed such legislation. Seven states have rejected putting similar laws in place. Bills are pending in other states; also there is legislation pending in the House and Senate. Additional information is available from www.freepress.net, including details of legislation pending in various states and letters being drafted by coalitions working to keep local Internet access open.

International Action

In September 2005, United Methodist Women were partners with the General Board of Global Ministries in a delegation that participated in the final session of the World Summit on the Information Society (WSIS), sponsored by the United Nations and organized by the International Telecommunications Union. The WSIS process, which involved governments, the business sector, and non-governmental organizations, provides an opportunity for concerned citizens from around the world to talk together about the impact of media and information technologies on their lives, and to highlight for governments critical justice issues in the future of information technologies and the right to communicate. In a conference that was dominated by the views of the communications industry, citizens' participation was absolutely essential to provide a voice to speak out on behalf of democratic and people-centered policies. Important actions at the local level can be possible as a follow-up to the WSIS conference, creating opportunities to translate the imperatives of the conference into realities at the local level.

Sign of Hope: Media Ownership Makes a Difference

Immokalee, Florida, April 2004

"...[C]onsciousness plus commitment equals change."

The Coalition of Immokalee Workers (CIW) announced that it would end its three-year boycott of the fast food chain Taco Bell in response to the company's pledge to fund a penny per pound increase that will go directly to workers. Taco Bell also agreed to work with the coalition to address the wages and working conditions of farm workers in Florida. CIW includes Mexican, Haitian, Guatemalan, and other immigrant workers who pick tomatoes, watermelons, cucumbers, and peppers.

In its long struggle for fair wages the Coalition enlisted the help of economic and social justice advocates around the United States. The United Methodist Church General Conference in 2004 voted to support the boycott. United Methodist Women participated in action to bring a peaceful settlement in March 2005. Critical to the CIW victory was the use of media and the Internet to publicize their campaign. "The boycott really got off the ground when we started to tell our own stories on the website."

But for CIW having a website was not enough: "...it's nothing without grassroots action." In order to accomplish this part of their struggle, the coalition set up a low power radio station. "We hope the radio station will bring us together, when we hear our own voices and really reach the local community."[53]

WCIW, launched in December 2003, is a low power FM station that operates in the ten-mile radius of the town of Immokalee, Florida. Staffed by community people, many of whom have been trained by WCIW, the station speaks with the voice of the community. The station uses live talk programming during peak morning and evening hours to reach the farm worker community with information about its organizing efforts and news about support received from other organizations. This helps farm workers to know that they are not alone in their struggle. "So when the endorsement of the boycott by The United Methodist Church happened, we could talk to people about that and really broadcast that to the community." Its commercial-free music programming includes both traditional and contemporary music of the home countries of the farm worker community. It is also able to link with Mexican and Guatemalan radio stations, and belongs to a bilingual network of community radio stations across the country.

Julia Perkins, CIW media staff, explained the philosophy of the station:

"The media work is based in our organizing formula—consciousness plus commitment equals change. So the media work is mostly focused on the question of consciousness—a basic consciousness about what is going on, who are the creators of these problems, and what we can do about them. In the community the idea has been to raise the consciousness of the workers about what their reality is, what the causes of the daily abuses that they face are, and how together we can combat that."[54]

Perkins explained that before the radio station opened, most of this work involved door-to-door contacts using flyers and video, trying to bridge the language divides of Spanish, Haitian Creole, and many indigenous languages from Guatemalan and southern Mexican workers, who all face the same situation in the fields. Each season a new group of farm workers arrive and the

Continued...

processes of consciousness raising must begin anew. It was almost impossible to reach everyone. With the radio station, CIW can enter into the homes of farm workers, to have conversations about such things as their legal rights and services available to them. After only six months on the air the station provided an important way to mobilize the community. In the aftermath of a hurricane, it was discovered that companies with government contracts were not paying Immokalee workers who were being used as laborers for the clean up. The station was able to broadcast this information and make a call for unpaid workers to meet. As a result of these efforts the head of the contracting company went to the community to deliver back pay personally to some 250 workers.

WCIW got its start with the help of Prometheus Radio, a Philadelphia-based community radio advocacy and technical assistance group. When WCIW received its license from the FCC three years after its application, Prometheus organized a "barn raising," recruiting radio professionals from around the country to go to Immokalee and help with the set up of the station and training of its staff.

WCIW serves the local area that was previously only served by a commercial Spanish-speaking station. In the past, WCIW worked with that station on a call-in program about workers rights, but CIW had to pay for the time. Perkins concluded: "The commercial radio stations are not about the community's needs."

Bangkok Postscript

August 2005 — The $10 million criminal libel suit against Supinya Klangnarong opened in Bangkok, Thailand. The defense case was dealt a setback when the judges upheld the Shin Corporation attorney's objection to interpreters (selected by Supinya's attorneys) for the Canadian and Filipino media expert witnesses scheduled to testify on her behalf. The defense had hoped to use the testimony of prominent journalists from other countries to point to international freedom of press standards including the discrediting of the kind of criminal defamation suit to which Supinya is being subjected.

A member of the Thai National Human Rights Commission testifying in the case reminded the judges of the many human rights treaties granting freedom of expression to which Thailand is a signatory.

The World Association of Christian Communication has condemned the criminal libel suit and gathered signatures for a petition that the suit be dropped. WACC has an ongoing weblog (http://www.wacc.org.uk/Supinya) that provides information on the case. ∎

Chapter 5 Challenging Economic Globalization —Building Global Community

"**O**ur faithfulness to God and to God's free gift of life compels us to confront idolatrous assumptions, unjust systems, with politics of domination and exploitation in the current world economic order. Economics and economic justice are always masters of faith as they touch the very core of God's will for creation."

—"Alternative Globalization Addressing Peoples and Earth,"
World Council of Churches, 2005

Since 1998, the World Council of Churches, its member denominations, Councils of Churches, and related organizations have been involved in a process to articulate "an ecumenical vision of life in just and loving relationships, through a search for alternatives to the present economic structures." This process, known as AGAPE (Alternative Globalization Addressing Peoples and Earth), has involved conversations and consultations at the local, national, regional, and global level. The process was built on the premise that "God of bounding grace and love...is a theological and spiritual basis...that challenges the churches to act....We act because we respond to God's admission of ushering in justice and peace on earth." [55]

All of the discussions involved many of the same topics that we have been considering: economic globalization, free trade, the work of the World Bank and the World Trade Organization, privatization, and investment. While there was a wide variety of rich and diverse discussion, there were several important points of agreement:

1. That the current model of economic globalization is causing serious harm throughout the world, particularly to the poor and the vulnerable;

2. That the promise of life abundant is a promise for the whole of humanity and creation;

3. That the treatment of the vulnerable is the measuring rod by which Christians judge economic policies.

These conversations echoed the experiences of the organizations and groups that we have been learning about in their struggle to overcome the injustices that they face as a result of economic globalization. We are surrounded by a large cloud of witnesses in our efforts to understand and accept the challenge of building global community. It must be said that this cloud of witnesses has been to some extent created by economic globalization, but even more important, enabled by the technologies for international contact that are part of globalization.

The task that lies before us is striving to be the change that we want to see. We will have to be able to work on all of the three dimensions that were the centerpiece of our picture of globalization's interconnections: resources, livelihoods, and communications.

Economic globalization touches our own personal lives: what we eat and drink and wear, what kinds of jobs we have, what our job security looks like, what social services we can expect, and what information shapes what we believe to be true and how we understand the world. The starting points for action are in the everyday spaces of our lives. We can think about whether it is absolutely necessary for us to drink bottled water, and we can work to make sure that access to clean and safe water remains under public control. We can try to be responsible shoppers, supporting cooperatives and fairly traded products. We can become media literate and advocate for media justice and accountability, making sure that all places and perspectives are heard.

We know that we need to look at our role as citizens and at the actions of the U.S. government. For U.S. citizens, this is perhaps the most complicated and difficult task. The strategies of privatization and deregulation affect not only persons living in the United States, but people all around the world. Our burden of responsibility is therefore quite heavy. In order to ensure a different and more just future, we need to consider matching the churches' excellent record for the provision of development assistance and social services to the poor and vulnerable, both inside the United States and in the rest of the world, with an equally vigorous pursuit of policy changes around issues of trade and investment.

The World Council of Churches process, *Christianity, Poverty and Wealth,* included the following comment: "There must be the rule of justice, not just the plea for it." We need to take a close look at the political language that is used in the discussion of economic policy. We must learn to recognize when words like democracy and freedom are used in ways that actually close down the ability to participate in the critical decisions that affect life, rather than opening them up; when the rights called for are the rights of the corporations over the rights of citizens. We must be prepared to act when we see the demands of militarism and the "war on terrorism" linked to the demands of market-driven economic policy and used to control Earth's weaker nations as a part of the promise of "aid."[56]

All of this means that we have to look again to our own values, and measure current economic policies that are bound up in what we have called economic globalization, in order to determine where we stand and what we must do. It will be important to separate the values inherited from our faith traditions from those that have been so much a part of the identity of U.S. citizens. We will need to reexamine ideas like competition and unlimited growth, as we have done in these pages, to see if they serve the purposes of bringing abundant life to all. We will need to think again about where to draw the line between abundant life and greed. Can we think about a line of greed that would be at the end of our understanding of the poverty line? We must seek to understand whether our faith imperative is harmonious with the idea that everything—including all of a person's materials and resources—is a commodity that can be bought and sold. And, because the entire economic globalization process is built on it, we will have to ultimately decide whether we think that the market rather than government should be the instrument for the will of the people.

* * * * *

As we go forward to meet the challenge of globalization, seeking to build a global community, we can pray that we will be able to affirm with the churches of Western Europe: "No one is excluded from God's household of life. The Christian community reflects this vision for the sake of the whole world. Guided by this vision, we strive for an economy in the service of life."[57]

Notes

CHAPTER 1

1. BBC World News, January 2005.

2. *United Nations Human Development Report*, 2004, http://hdr.undp.org/reports.

3. Kofi Annan, in General Conference Resolution 309. "Globalization and Its Impact on Human Dignity and Human Rights," *The Book of Resolutions, 2004*, p. 773.

4. Amartya Sen, *Development as Freedom*. Anchor Books, New York, 1999, p.18.

5. General Conference Resolution 309 (see note 3), pp. 784-785.

6. Ibid., p. 774.

CHAPTER 2

7. Ada Kidd, "Drinking Water," *Response*, November 2004, pp. 28-31.

8. www.fijiwater.com.

9. Telephone interview with Virisila Buadromo, Executive Director, Fiji Women's Rights Movement, April 9, 2005.

10. Ibid.

11. Ibid.

12. *Response*, November 2004.

13. www.citizen.org/cmep/Water/articles.cfm?ID=9749.

14. www.house.gov/schakowsky/WaterForTheWorld.html.

15. Interview with Linda Schramm, April 2005.

16. Telephone interview with Ann Whiting, *Michigan Christian Advocate*, July 12, 2005; and telephone interview with Ada Kidd, Environmental Justice Coordinator for the Michigan Area United Methodist Church, August 29, 2005.

CHAPTER 3

17. Eddie Gordon, Southern Shrimp Alliance Press Release, November 30, 2004.

18. Telephone interview with Deborah Long, Public Relations, Southern Shrimp Alliance, March 2005.

19. Russ Henderson, "Feds Uphold Tariffs Sought by Shrimpers," Everything Alabama, www.al.com, Tuesday, December 21, 2004.

Notes (continued)

20. Interview with Vera Moore, UMW member, Mobile, Alabama, March 2005; and telephone interview with Myra Sutton, UMW member, Bayou La Batre, Alabama, April 2005.

21. Action Aid, www.actionaid.org/vietnam.

22. www.actionaid.org/vietnam/1033_3_1292.html.

23. www.actionaid.org/vietnam.

24. Deborah Long interview (see note 18).

25. Radley Balko, "Trade & Protectionism, Big Shrimp," www.abetterearth.org/article.php?id=882.

26. www.actionaid.org/vietnam.

27. Linda Levine, "Offshoring (a.k.a. Offshore Outsourcing) and Job Insecurity Among U.S. Workers," Congressional Research Service, updated May 2, 2005, http://fpc.state.gov/documents/organization/46688.pdf.

28. Ibid.

29. Sarah Anderson and John Cavanagh, "Outsourcing: A Policy Agenda," Foreign Policy in Focus, Policy Brief Vol. 9, No. 2, April 2004, www.fpif.org/briefs/vol9/v9n02outsource.html.

30. *Principles for Global Corporate Responsibility: Benchmarks for Measuring Business Performance.* Third Edition, Revised and Released 2003, Steering Group of the Global Principles Network, www.bench-marks.org.

31. Kathy Jumper, "Condo fever hits Causeway," *Mobile Register,* June 5, 2005.

32. Russ Henderson, "Developer Seeks Bayou land—Bayou La Batre condos on the Bayou?" *Mobile Register,* March 30, 2005.

33. Russ Henderson, "Lipscomb blesses fleet in Bayou, Feeling Blessed," *Mobile Register,* May 2, 2005.

34. "Sound Off," *Mobile Register,* May 3, 2005.

35. Matt Apuzzo, "Hurricane Damage May Doom Gulf's Shrimp Industry," *The Tampa Tribune,* September 15, 2005.

CHAPTER 4

36. *CIA World Fact Books.* www.cia.gov/cia/publications/factbook/geos/th.html.

37. www.wacc.org.uk.

38. www.wacc.org.uk.

39. From the *Thai Post*, July 16, 2003, www.wacc.org.uk.

40. Interview with Taishi Duchicela, Media Justice Advocate for Youth Media Council, May 2005.

41. www.youthmediacouncil.org/publications.html.

42. www.clearchannel.com.

43. Interview with Taishi Duchicela (see note 39).

44. Ibid.

45. Ibid.

46. Roberto Verzola, "Lords of Cyberspace," http://mail.kein.org/pipermail/incom-l/2004-April/000052.html.

47. *Alternative Globalization Addressing Peoples and Earth (AGAPE), A Background Document*, World Council of Churches, April 2005.

48. www.mediachannel.org.

49. Fact Sheet: " 'Digital Divide' Widening at Lower Income Levels—Falling Through the Net: Defining the Digital Divide," November 1999.

50. "Digital Divide Will Right Itself, Report Says," eGovmonitor News Desk, September 5, 2005, www.egovmonitor.com/node/2551.

51. Gal Beckerman, "Tripping Up Big Media," *Columbia Journalism Review*, Issue 6: November/December 2003, p.8, www.cjr.org/issues/2003/6/media-beckerman.asp.

52. www.ucc.org/ocinc/mep/orgman.htm.

53. Interview with Julia Perkins, Media Staff, Coalition of Immokalee Workers, August 2005.

54. Ibid.

CHAPTER 5

55. *AGAPE Background Document,* Foreword (see note 47).

56. Michael Taylor, *Christianity, Poverty and Wealth—The Findings of "Project 21,"* World Council of Churches.

57. *AGAPE Background Document* (see note 47).

Study Guide

Introduction and Overview

Why a Mission Study on Globalization?

You may be asking yourself, why in the world would we need to have a mission study on globalization? After all, what can all that information about economics and markets possibly have to do with the life of ordinary people in local communities? How can we make sense of the many confusing and complex aspects related to those fields? Of course, globalization is everywhere all around us. It affects us every time we go online to use the Internet or make a transaction on an ATM machine instead of going inside the bank. We're affected when we hear a foreign correspondent thousands of miles away report on a war that is being fought or a disaster that needs assistance. Globalization is reflected in the increasing variety and diversity of the people who live in our communities and in the private company from whom we now receive our water bills. No one asked us if we wanted any of these changes, it was somehow happening before we knew it. So globalization is a reality, and we as Christians need to understand what it's about, what role

we can play in the important decisions, and what has been happening to shape our values while we were not paying attention. At the outset it's important to say that this mission study is not a study for economists. A degree in economics will not be necessary in order to benefit from, participate in, and shape this study. The purposes for this study are simple: we want to look at the economic policies that are shaping our world; we want to understand the values that those economic policies are promoting; and we want to use the yardstick of our faith to help us to decide how to relate to, influence, and change those policies where changes are needed.

This study is grounded in the idea that there are no magic or right answers to the questions of how to build a just global economic system. This study encourages thinking about very complex realities. It will be difficult because current global economic policies are connected to large international events and tied to the realities of the identity of the United States and its power, particularly since 1990 and the dissolution of the Soviet Union. That event has been widely interpreted as the victory of capitalism and democracy over communism and totalitarianism. As a result, a set of economic policies has risen to ascendency, policies rooted in an interpretation of capitalism that insists that the market can solve all problems. This situation is particularly complicated for U.S. citizens because it also suggests that somehow capitalism and democracy are the same thing. So as we embark on the study of globalization we will be haunted by a sub-theme: what kind of economic system is necessary in order for democracy, one of our cherished institutions, to flourish?

A compelling reason for a mission study on globalization is that in a very real sense, the future of the world is at stake. If we as Christians are to respond to God's action on behalf of justice in the world, we cannot but take seriously the reality of globalization in the world today. As a facilitator of this study, you need to keep in mind the importance of acknowledging that there are many things about globalization that are threatening to life as we have known it, that challenge our values, and that cause us to feel unsettled and to live perhaps in fear. If we are to understand globalization and learn how to challenge it where it needs to be challenged, we have to be able to recognize these fears.

What is Globalization?

As you undertake to facilitate this study of globalization, keep in mind the central idea that globalization has many faces and uses facts related to very complex phenomena. As learners, we all like to resist the idea of complexity. We would prefer simple information and simple answers to all questions. Unfortunately, globalization does not give us

this option. The contention of this study is that understanding that very complexity makes it possible for us to respond in the diverse ways that are necessary to take part in God's action in history. At the heart of globalization is a series of economic strategies that do not just affect economic realities, they also impact the environment, cultures, our consumption, and the way we are able to live.

The Lessons of the Good Samaritan

For this study we will focus our attention on the story of the Good Samaritan as recorded in Luke 10. We have chosen this text because in it Jesus offers us practical advice about how to live the faithful life. The text recognizes that everything is not always wonderful in the world—bad things happen. It acknowledges that there is diversity in the world, that all people are not the same. The text also recognizes that people who claim to follow the path of religion do not always respond to difficulty in the faithful way. We can get caught up in other people's troubles and have to figure out what to do. It therefore seems a fitting metaphor for the current reality. It is a story that lets us peel away many layers to discover new understanding. While on the surface it appears that this is a story of a group of individuals, it actually provides a lesson for how to deal with the whole world. As a facilitator, take time to read this passage and to reflect on how it can apply when a neighbor is the neighborhood. Think about what it means to give assistance to a person of another race or ethnic group or to receive assistance from a person of another race or ethnic group. In using this study we hope to explore the idea of what it might mean to think about the world as the beloved community.

Basic Learning Strategies

The learning strategies for this study guide are designed to be harmonious with the strategies of the book itself. This study guide provides an opportunity to pick and choose some elements of the book and to fashion them into a collective learning experience. The book is meant to provide you as a facilitator with the raw material for crafting a learning experience particularly suited to the group with which you will be working. As you are leading the sessions, be careful to learn which parts of the globalization story are most interesting to your learners. Use those points of interest as the heart of the learning experience that you are trying to create.

Globalization Times

The heart of the structure of the book is a series of stories from real life called "Globalization Times," which are literally stories taken from the headlines. Each chapter of the book begins with these stories. The aim of these stories is to help readers and learners place themselves in the middle of the globalization picture. The stories are taken from many parts of the world, but the hope is that in each story readers and learners will see something of their own experience or the experience of someone they know. The paired stories that begin Chapters 2, 3, and 4 reflect similar realities in different parts of the world. They also attempt to reflect the value contradictions that are key to understanding the reality of globalization.

Journaling Reflections

In each chapter the learner is asked to think about and identify important elements in each story and the similarities between the two stories. This is the place where the connection between the global and the local and between experiences and values is first made. Learners should be encouraged to record on journaling pages their reactions to the stories and their understanding of what is happening in those stories. This is a way for learners to take an active role in their own learning process.

Basic Facts, Charts, and Definitions

Each chapter has a number of charts, graphs, and diagrams that are designed to add new information about some of the global and national realities behind the stories. These materials should serve as resources for you as you organize the material for each session. Two diagrams, "Globalization Interconnections" and "Negotiating the Global Commons," should be used as worksheets for helping to identify the players in the stories and to explore possible action responses.

Biblical Reflection

Continuing reflections on the Luke 10 story of the Good Samaritan are important in working out ways to understand and imagine new solutions to the problems and opportunities created by globalization. Each chapter includes an opportunity for reflection on this text, with particular reference to the problems that are being addressed in the chapter. The idea is to bring the story of the Good Samaritan into the present in order to help us understand its relevance for our lives. Some of the questions we want to answer are:

- Who are the characters?
- How do we view ourselves and those controlling our economies?

- How is the road in this story a metaphor for the paths we must travel in the contemporary world?

- How are the experience of robbery and the responses of apathy and compassion metaphors for things that go on in our own communities?

- How can we use our rereading of the story of the Good Samaritan to help us envision a new economy for the global community that God intends?

General Conference Statements on Social Principles and Ecumenical Statements

Make use of statements on the issues of global economy from the General Conference and other church-related sources. These statements should become a central focal point for all discussions around the relationship of globalization to the responsibilities of faith. If these statements are easily visible they can be a kind of yardstick that is referred to from time to time as the group gets into the more controversial and paradoxical aspects of the reality of globalization. The session plans suggest printing these statements on large paper and posting them around your classroom or reproducing them as handouts. The statements are excellent sources for reflections by your group and will also help in the development of action strategies.

What Can Be Done? and Sign of Hope

Each chapter gives the learners an opportunity to think about solutions to the problems posed by the two stories. Here the learners have the chance to entertain alternative solutions to the problems of economic globalization. This section concludes with some concrete examples of strategies that are being used by others to work on the problems that have been identified. The chapters conclude with examples of other stories from real-life people and communities dealing with and transforming some of the basic problems of globalization into new and creative possibilities.

Additional Learning Strategies

Games and Exercises

While the issue of the global economy is definitely serious, the study should also be fun. Exploring difficult context is much easier when it is also enjoyable, and when it makes use of many modes of learning. This study guide contains a number of games and exercises that can make the sessions more engaging, offering people the opportunity to move around and play a little with some of these very difficult and challenging ideas. These games and exercises also help to reinforce the idea that each person can bring something to the discussion. Everyone teaches and everyone learns.

Worship

Ideally, the elements of worship should grow out of the life of the learning group. The worship center that will be described in more detail later should include symbols and materials that are relevant to the concerns of your particular group of learners. The experience of worship should be an opportunity to celebrate God's action in the midst of globalization, to confess our own complicity in injustice, and to make new commitments for transformation. Encourage the members of your group to take responsibility for the development of worship in each session. This study guide will suggest general themes and give possibilities for worship, but it will be up to the members of your group to construct worship appropriate to their discussion and their concerns.

Preparing for the Study

Reflect on Your Own Experience

The best way to begin preparations for this study might be simply to reflect on your own experiences. Write down how globalization has affected your life. Share these reflections with your group at the beginning of the study. It is very important that your group understands your perspectives on the study and why you want to be a part of facilitating their discussions and their learning.

Expand Your Perspective

After establishing this baseline, review the text. Read other books that reflect your interest or the interests you anticipate the group will have. See the Resources (p. 161) for a list of print and web resources with helpful suggestions.

Develop Session Plans

The best advice for planning your sessions is *choose* and *adapt*. Select those materials from the book and the study guide that are most useful for your own group. Adapt any of the suggested charts, exercises, or Bible studies to the particular needs of your group. Develop your own plan for sessions based upon your interest in the things that are most important in this study. You may want to develop some other features for each session; for example, bringing a news clipping about globalization, or asking others to bring news items, so that you're continually making the study not just academic but relevant and up-to-the-minute. This challenges participants to experience globalization as alive and working each day in every moment in their lives.

Chart Interconnections

Perhaps the single most important thing is seeing the interconnections between people, nations, and economic policies. You may want to chart some of those interconnections for yourself, or make your own annotations on the interconnections charts in each chapter of the book, in order to establish the beginning point for your discussions with your group.

Establish the Learning Environment

Make the learning environment as comfortable as possible for your group, perhaps by placing chairs in a circle or setting up tables for small group work. Think of ways to make the group feel physically and emotionally comfortable and affirmed in the course of their study.

- **Print some key statements and concepts and post them around the room.** This is another way to stimulate the learning environment and to make information available for easy reference.

- **Display pictures from around the world.** Since the study focuses on connections, the more your group can visualize people and other parts of the world, the easier it will be to understand and expand on your discussion of the connections. As resources for pictures, use back issues of *Response* and *New World Outlook* magazines. These publications always feature stories from other parts of the world and highlight some of the kinds of problems that will be discussed in this study. Create a montage of pictures on poster board or a bulletin board, or scatter pictures around the room in order to stimulate learning. If possible, choose pictures that relate specifically to the places discussed in the text. If you communicate with class members beforehand, invite them to bring pictures that exemplify globalization.

Shared Leadership

Involve everyone in both learning and teaching by sharing group leadership with participants. The strategy of learning for this study is that everyone can understand the global economy in which everyone is living. So finding ways to continue to affirm the basic facts of the study will be very important to the success of the study.

Plan Time Carefully

Since there are so many things to talk about, careful planning ensures that you will have sufficient time for each activity. But one in-depth discussion is better than three discussions that are only able to scratch the surface. Monitor how a discussion is going so you can decide when to lead a discussion on and when to cut it off and move to another part of your work. The study guide will include suggestions for the time for particular activities, but you will really need to judge this for yourself.

Alternative Learning Plans

Many groups in local church settings or conference schools do not have an eight-hour block of time available for learning. The following are some suggested alternative learning plans:

Six Hours

Session 1: two hours
Session 2 or 3: two hours
Session 4: two hours

Two Hours

Session 1 or 3

One Hour

Session 1: "Introducing Ourselves and Our Global Connections," "Sharing Our Knowledge About Economic Globalization," Bible Study, Worship

Session 1

Our study of globalization must begin with ourselves. We need to use ourselves as a resource—our political and economic lives and also our lives as people of faith. It is important at the outset to understand and share within the group our individual experiences of globalization, and through that process to build the shared collective understanding of globalization as the beginning point for learning together. The first session affirms our own knowledge and the value of that knowledge for building a more complex understanding. It is also important in this session to recognize that our knowledge is based not only on both positive and negative experiences, but also on attitudes, prejudices, and emotional responses to many events that are going on in our world. The foundation built in this first session will be critical to the success of the study. One of its outcomes should be that all learners identify themselves as "experts on globalization."

Goals:

- To introduce ourselves and share experiences of globalization.
- To create a baseline of common understanding.
- To explore what we know about globalization, both positive and negative.
- To identify what we have at stake in globalization.

Materials and Supplies:

- copies of the text for each participant
- Bibles
- hymnals (see suggested hymns)
- prepared newsprint sheets (see Preparation)
- world map (such as *Peters Projection Map*)
- pictures from around the world (see back issues of *Response* and *New World Outlook* magazines)
- small (2" x 2") self-adhesive notepads, large colorful dots (several colors)
- 3" x 5" index cards
- handout of story of the Good Samaritan (in several translations, if possible)
- votive candles (two for each participant)

Preparation:

- **Write down your own expectations, fears, and questions** about globalization. Reflect on and pray about them. Immerse yourself in your own understandings and concerns about globalization.
- **Reread the Introduction and Chapter 1** in the book, as well as taking some time to study and reflect on the story of the Good Samaritan in Luke.
- **Arrange chairs in a circle.** Push tables out of the way to create plenty of room in the middle for activities requiring movement.

- **Display a good world map or large globe.** The *Peters Projection Map* is a valuable resource, available from the Service Center.

- **Display pictures from around the world** from magazines or newspapers.

- **Prepare and display newsprint sheets.** Print the following on large sheets:

  - **The overall goals and study design, plus the design and goals for Session 1.** Members of the group need to know what to expect. Consider leaving additional space for the members of your group to add their own ideas and concerns. Continue to display these sheets for the group to refer to throughout the study. You may also want to duplicate your overall study plan and goals as a handout.

  - **The basic ground rules for interaction of members of the group.** Include suggestions about confidentiality, respect for others, not interrupting other people, and so forth. These should also be in draft form, with additional space for group input.

  - **"The Parking Lot."** Also prepare a sheet titled "The Parking Lot." This is a place to note any questions or ideas that need further group discussion.

  - **Comment Sheets.** Post some blank newsprint sheets for class members to record random comments that they may wish to make about the study, the materials, each other, or the process. This provides an opportunity for people to reflect on the study and their experience of the study. This is an important avenue of feedback for you as the facilitator, and could reveal problems that need to be solved or adjustments to be made to the schedule.

  - **General Conference Statements.** Specifically for this session, post the quotations about a just global economy from General Conference Resolutions 206 and 208 (Appendix, pp. 148-149).

- **Prepare handouts.** The story of the Good Samaritan will be used many times in the course of this study. Encourage the members of your group to bring their Bibles to read the text from the Bible. You may wish to duplicate the text as a handout so that participants can make notes in the margin and write questions to use in more informal ways than they would be able to do with their own Bibles. If possible, make handouts using several different translations.

- **Gather self-stick notepads or colored dots.** For the opening exercises of this session you'll need to have either small (2" x 2") sticky notepads or large colorful dots that class members can use to place on the map. Several colors of both the sticky pads and the dots will come in handy for quickly getting down to and sharing ideas on different subjects.

- **Make a large drawing of a car** to post in the front of the room, or simulate a car by setting up two rows of two chairs each. Prepare the following name signs for different actors in economic globalization: transnational corporations, farmers, blue-collar workers, white-collar workers, China, World Bank, World Trade Organization, unions, local communities, big investors, and so forth. As a reference for this exercise, use the charts: "Understanding Global Investment" (p. 34), "The Global Corporation" (p. 34), and "What's Global" (pp. 84-85). They can also serve as references for your learners during this exercise.

- **On a chalk board or dry erase board, print the following:**

"On the 3" x 5" card, write down one thing that you hope to gain from participation in the globalization study, one question you hope to have answered, or one concern that you have about globalization."

Introducing Ourselves and Our Global Connections (15 minutes)

1. Expectation Cards

As learners enter, hand out several 3" x 5" cards. Call the attention of participants to the instructions on the board, and invite them to jot down their responses on the cards. Once everyone is present you're ready to begin the study.

2. Personal Introductions

Say that in order to get to know one another better and to begin the building of joint knowledge about globalization, the first activity is self-introduction—sharing some information about the connection that each person has to another part of the world and locating that place on the map. Demonstrate how this activity will be carried out by introducing yourself. Designate one color of dot for family connections, another color for work connections, another color for consumer connections, and another color for political connections. For example, as the facilitator of the group I would say: "My name is elmira and my husband was from South Africa," and then I would place a blue dot on the map on South Africa. Any kind of connection to another part of the world makes for useful introductions: working for a company with factories in other parts of the world; liking coffee grown in another part of the world; using the Internet; wearing clothes made in another country; adopting a child from another country.

Once all the introductions have been made, ask the group to take a brief moment for reflection on what they think it means that the group has so many connections to other parts of the world.

Introduce the Study (15 minutes)

3. Clarifying Goals

Walk the group through the list of goals for the study that you have prepared. Once the list has been read, ask them if they have questions or anything they would like to add to the list. Remind them to refer to the cards they filled out at the beginning of the class to see if anything on those cards needs to be added to the list of goals for this study. This will ensure that the goals are a good reflection of what group members actually feel they personally need to get out of the study.

Follow a similar process to discuss the broad plan for the sessions of the study with the group. It's important to let them see how their discussions will proceed and what issues will be covered in the course of the study. Check with the group to make sure they feel comfortable with the plan and that the plan for this study meets their needs. You should be prepared for the possibility that you will need to make some adjustments to the study plan in order to accommodate those additional needs that you can meet, that would enhance the group's overall satisfaction with the study.

4. Discuss Ground Rules

Begin with the list of possible ground rules that you prepared in advance, but also give group members a chance to add additional items.

Participants can revisit the ground rules to help solve some interpersonal problems that may arise during the course of the study. This process of allowing the group to develop and affirm the overall rules, rather than having the rules imposed, is very likely to enhance the learning that goes on within your group.

Learning Activities

5. Sharing Our Knowledge About Economic Globalization (20 minutes)

This exercise builds on the earlier introductions but begins to pinpoint specifically the effects of economic globalization, and lays the groundwork for identifying some of the sources of power that determine those policies. Ask the group to stand in a circle and then give the following instruction to the group: "Listen as I read the following statements. If a statement is true for you, take one step forward toward the center. Then look at who is with you.

"Step forward if you:

- Know of a family or a community that has lost jobs or suffered wage cuts because corporations moved to another community in the United States or outside the United States, or because of corporate competition;
- Have lost your job or someone in your family has lost a job due to corporate downsizing;
- Are wearing an article of clothing made in another country or eat fruits and vegetables grown in another country;
- Know someone who has been affected by health care Medicare cutbacks;
- Shop at Wal-Mart and are able to take advantage of the lower price of imported goods;
- Live in a rural community that now has a growing immigrant population;

- Belong to a union that has lost much of its bargaining power;
- Live in a small community that has recently acquired a new prison operated by a private corporation that has increased local employment;
- Are worried about plans to shift Social Security to private accounts;
- Work for a corporation that employs people in more than one country;
- Wonder if there can be such a thing as jobless economic recovery;
- Wonder why corporations like Halliburton are involved in so much of the rebuilding work in Iraq."

Feel free to add to and delete from this list to make it as relevant as possible for your group. Ask group members to suggest additional situations.

Once you have completed all of the movements in the exercise, take five minutes to ask the group to reflect on what conclusions we can draw from globalization and its collective effect on us. Those who made the most advance toward the center are those that globalization has touched most closely. On a large newsprint sheet, make a note of some of the actors that are identified; what group members perceive to be the role of government; which aspects of globalization they feel are problematic; and which aspects they feel represent possibilities.

Break (10 minutes)

6. Who Is Driving the Car? (20 minutes)

Call participants' attention to the car drawing or the four chairs simulating the seats of a car. Explain that the idea of the exercise is to identify where different actors are located in the power processes of economic globalization. There are some who are in the driver's seat controlling many things, there are others who are perhaps along for the ride, and maybe some others are getting run over.

Hand out the identity placards based on players identified in Chapter 1. Ask group members to come forward to put each identity in the place that represents its role or power position in the engine of the global economy. Ask the group to refer to the charts "Understanding Global Investment," "The Global Corporation," and "What's Global," and to think of other actors in the drama. As each name card is placed in, under, or around the car, class members must explain why they feel that person or institution is in that particular place in relationship to globalization. Once all the actors have been placed, talk together about why the picture looks as it does. See if the group can come to a consensus about power relationships and who are the winners and losers in economic globalization.

- Who are the most powerful and who seems to have little or no power?
- How are power relationships changing?

Now invite group members to try to place themselves in the car. Where are they or their interests represented? Have them print their names on extra index cards or self-stick notes and place them in the car.

If you made a drawing of the car, display it in the classroom as an additional reference for your discussions. If you used chairs, make a chart to display, indicating where class members placed themselves (driver's seat, passenger seat, along for the ride, being run over, and so forth).

7. Bible Study: Luke 10 (20 minutes)

Before reading the Good Samaritan text, put the passage in context. Point out that this text is part of a block of material in the gospel that extends from Luke 9:51 to 19:28, events that take place as Jesus is traveling to Jerusalem. In general, Jesus gives some practical advice about the qualities needed by the faithful leading up to this story, or advice on how to live the faithful life.

Invite members of your group to read Luke 10 using different translations in order to see some slightly different interpretations of the text. Ask for a volunteer to record on newsprint some key elements of this discussion so that over the course of the study the group will see their understanding of the text of the Good Samaritan grow.

ASK:

- Who are the players in this story?
- How could the story of the Good Samaritan be a metaphor for globalization?

Ask the group to reflect particularly on the role of the Good Samaritan himself as a person of a different racial/ethnic group and the role of the innkeeper who became part of the collective responsibility for caring for the injured person.

Worship—God's Transforming Power (15 minutes)

Tell participants that it is important to bring into a worship context the concerns about economic globalization that have been raised during this session. Even the most secular economic concerns are relevant to bring into the context of worship. As people of faith we must continually recenter ourselves within our understanding of God's power and God's action in the world.

Call to Worship

Leader: Holy God, we gather before you this day as your people beginning a journey of learning.

People: **Open our hearts and minds to recognize the signs of your transforming power at work in our world,**

Leader: That power which continues to feed the hungry, clothe the naked, free the oppressed, and break every yoke.

People: **Help us to hear the voices of others whose lives are impacted by globalization even as we struggle with our own feelings of powerlessness in the midst of its powerful forces.**

All: **Fill us with your Holy Spirit, Teacher God. Help us to recommit ourselves as a covenant community to working for a global economic order that manifests Gospel values.**

Suggested Hymn

"We Are Called" (*The Faith We Sing,* #2172)

Scripture

Luke 10:25-37, The Good Samaritan

Time of Intercession: Lighting of the Candles of Hope and Struggle

Leader: Knowing that all is in the hands of God, we pause now to recall and place in the context of prayer all that we have talked about today. Let us pray.

All: **Oh God, we light these candles to recall those who suffer and struggle because powerful economic forces care more for profits and acquiring wealth than they do for the health and well-being of families and communities. We commend them to your continuing care.**

Members of the group are invited to come forward and light a candle sharing a remembrance of some of those mentioned in the discussion and concern for those who suffer and struggle. After all who wish to have spoken, the collective response is:

All: **We pray that you will keep us mindful of our commitment to their struggle. We light these candles to celebrate God's gift of connectedness that globalization also makes visible in our world.**

Members of the group are invited to come forward and light a candle sharing some of the examples of connectedness that were learned about during the session. When all who wish to have spoken the collective response is:

All: **May these lights keep us mindful of your transforming power in the world and the possibility of the building of a worldwide beloved community.**

Suggested Hymn

"We Are Marching" (*The Faith We Sing,* #2235) or "Let There Be Light" (*United Methodist Hymnal,* #440)

Closing Prayer

Close with a prayer of your own or ask a volunteer to close with prayer.

Assignments for Session 2 (5 minutes)

Ask the group to read Chapter 2 and then to make a list of the resources that are critical to the survival of their families and community. Encourage them to use this journaling time to write down any reflections they have on the idea of global resources. Point out that there will be a few minutes to share these reflections at the beginning of the next session.

Session 2

Basic resources like water, oil, natural gas, air, and food are necessary for survival. Economic globalization views all resources as commodities to be bought and sold. Survival is transformed from a basic right of a human being to something to be decided on the basis of the ability to pay. This applies to individuals, communities, and nations. In this session we will use one resource—water—to explore the implications of this economic strategy.

Goals:

• To show the impact of globalization on local resources.

• To explore the issues of privatization and governance.

• To open a discussion about a global resource commons.

• To think about our own consumption patterns and resources.

Materials and Supplies:

• prepared newsprint sheets (see Preparation)

• copies of "The Global Corporation" (p. 34), "Understanding Global Investment" (p. 34), "Water Privatization Picture" (p. 37), "Trading Services" (p. 38), "Globalization Interconnections—Resources" (Appendix, p. 150), and "Negotiating the Global Commons: Resources" (Appendix, p. 144) for each participant

• sheets of colored construction paper and markers

• symbols of water, soil, and food for Worship Center

• two votive candles per participant and matches

• Bibles and hymnals for each participant

Preparation:

• This session includes some theater exercises, so the room will need to have maximum flexibility. Arrange several separate small areas to facilitate small group discussion. Clear a space in the middle of the room big enough for four or five actors to present their portrayals.

• Familiarize yourself with the explanation and purposes of the "Forum Theatre" (Appendix, p. 151).

• Make extra copies of "The Global Corporation" (p. 34), "Understanding Global Investment" (p. 34), "Water Privatization Picture" (p. 37), "Trading Services" (p. 38), and "Globalization Interconnections—Resources" (Appendix, p. 150) for participants to use for note taking.

• Make extra copies of "Negotiating the Global Commons: Resources" (Appendix, p. 144) so that during the theater exercises class members can use these sheets to record some of their ongoing discussion.

• Rearrange the items on the table in the Worship Center. Include symbols that represent resource elements like water, soil, and food so those concerns are reflected in the worship service. You may want to choose a member of the group to prepare the Worship Center for the day rather than doing it yourself. Be sure to check the candles used in Session 1 to see if any need to be replenished.

- On a large sheet of newsprint paper, print and post Social Principles 160, "The Natural World" (quoted at the beginning of Chapter 2).

- Print a brief outline of the goals and process for this lesson. For the discussion of assignments at the end of the session, prepare a list of the potential actors in globalization that will be part of the following day's discussion. Wait until the end of the session to post this list, just in time for the discussion.

- For the introduction, prepare a newsprint sheet with two columns—one to identify resources and the second to identify who controls each resource.

- Recruit someone to read aloud the story of the Good Samaritan.

Opening Activities

1. Introduction (10 minutes)

Ask a few members of the group to share their written reflections on resources that are important to their lives. Record their responses on the newsprint sheet you prepared.

2. Bible Meditation (10 minutes)

This exercise provides a different approach to the Good Samaritan text. During this session we will be using this story of the Good Samaritan as a metaphor to help us understand the impact of globalization on resources and what can be done about it. The Bible meditation will provide a quiet space for the group to hear again this story of the Good Samaritan and to think deeply and prayerfully about its meaning in the contemporary context. As you

begin, ask the group members to recall the previous discussion of this story of the Good Samaritan as a metaphor for our life in the midst of globalization. Call attention to any notes that may be posted that were taken from that discussion. Ask members of the group to close their eyes and try to visualize the traveler in the story of the Good Samaritan, not as a person but as a resource in danger. Ask a member of the group to read slowly and clearly the full text of the story of the Good Samaritan, to pause, and then to read it a second time. This should be a quiet time with space for silent reflection.

Learning Activities

3. Forum Theatre Exercises: Community Resources in Danger (30-35 minutes)

Give the participants a brief explanation of the origin and purpose of "Forum Theatre" (Appendix, p. 151). This activity gives the group a chance to consider a number of possible strategies and the outcomes of those strategies that would be needed in order to protect local resources.

Explain that they will be divided into groups that will focus on thinking about how globalization affects particular local resources that are important for survival. The reason for using this approach is to help us consider the variety of perspectives that are involved and not just one "truth." These exercises also help us understand that these issues are not just intellectual but also emotional and spiritual. Point to the list that was developed in the introductory activity.

Divide the group into small groups with no more than four or five persons in each group. The groups might be divided on the basis of the resource in which each person is most interested or groups could simply be formed randomly. Remind group members that they should have on hand for the exercise the resources from Chapter 2 in the text. Issues of food are also addressed in Chapter 3. Where information is not available in the text, group members can fill in this basic structure of power relations from their own knowledge. The details are not as important in this exercise as working with the basic concepts.

Ask each group to identify a player in the resource situation that they have chosen as they imagine how the local reality corresponds to the dynamics of the story of the Good Samaritan.

- Who are the followers of the religion of globalization?

- Who are the robbers?

- Is there is a Samaritan?

- How do race and class dynamics come into play in the local resource reality?

Allow about 15 minutes to have this discussion. The task is to imagine that the local community is the Samaritan and to propose a way to address the problem. They need to be able to name the characters in the local situation and assign group members to play those roles in addition to determining the solutions that would model protecting resources for all. The idea is not to rehearse but to discuss what would happen and then be prepared to improvise the scene. Give each group sheets of construction paper on which to write the names of all the players in their drama, so members of the group will be able to follow the improvisation more easily.

After about 15 or 20 minutes, bring the group back together and ask for volunteers to come to the front and improvise their situation. Hand out copies of "Negotiating the Global

Commons: Resources," and ask members of the group to use these sheets for making notes about possible alternative solutions to the one that is being improvised. Each improvisation should be three to five minutes, so there should be time for two or three groups before the break.

Break (10 minutes)

4. Forum Theatre Exercises Continued (30-35 minutes)

Give the remaining groups the opportunity to present their improvisations. Once all the improvisations have been done consider each improvisation in turn.

ASK:

- Would the solutions suggested have the effect of protecting the endangered resources?

- Does anyone in any other group have another idea about how those resources might be protected (for example, involvement of other actors in the situation)?

Ask the group involved to return to the front of the room, and have the person who has the suggestion take over as the person portraying the local community and quickly improvise the new solution. These new improvisations should be no more than two minutes. Continue the activity for as long as you have time.

5. Wrap Up: Global Commons: Resources— What's Important (10 minutes)

Using the "Negotiating the Global Commons: Resources" worksheet again, ask the members of the groups to suggest additions and amendments to the worksheet based on their forum theatre experiences. Are there other resources that need to be added?

Worship—Celebrating God's Gifts of Resources, Commitment to Protection and Sharing (10 minutes)

The worship experience is designed to bring the discussion of the session into sacred space in order to make these concerns about economic globalization and our lives a part of the group's prayer life.

Call to Worship

All: Come, let us give thanks to God; for God is good and God's steadfast love endures forever;

Voice 1: who alone does great wonders,

Voice 2: who by understanding made the heavens,

Voice 3: who spread out the earth on the waters,

Voice 4: who made the great lights:

Voice 5: the sun to rule over the day,

Voice 6: the moon and stars to rule over the night.

All: God's steadfast love endures forever;

Voice 8: God remembers us in our low estate,

Voice 9: and rescues us from our foes,

Voice 10: and gives food to all flesh.

All: Come, let us give thanks to the God of heaven, for God's steadfast love endures forever.

> —Psalm 136, adapted

Intercession: Lighting the Candles of Struggle in Celebration

Leader: Knowing that everything is in the hands of God, we pause to recall and place in the context of prayer all that we have experienced today. Let us pray.

All: We light these candles to recall and pray for all those in local communities who in the face of the powerful forces of privatization and direct investment, struggle to preserve and protect local resources so that they might be shared by all.

Members of the group are invited to come forward and to light a candle. They can share a remembrance of those who were mentioned in the discussion and a concern for those who suffer and struggle. After all who wish to do so have spoken, the collective response is:

All: We offer these lights and these prayers as evidence of our commitment to share and protect resources for basic survival.

We light these candles to celebrate the mighty gifts of God of bountiful resources for our planet.

Members of the group are invited to come forward and light a candle, sharing some examples from the session of the bountiful resources that should be available for all. When all who wish to have spoken, the collective response is:

All: We offer these lights and these prayers as a testimony to God's magnificent gifts in this world and our responsibility to celebrate and share those gifts.

Suggested Hymns

"For the Beauty of the Earth (*United Methodist Hymnal* #92); "Wounded World that Cries for Healing" (*The Faith We Sing*, #2177); "I Am Your Mother" (*The Faith We Sing*, #2059)

Closing Prayer

Pray a closing prayer of your own choosing, or invite a participant to close with prayer.

Assignment (5 minutes)

Make copies of the "Globalization Reality" scenarios (Appendix, pp. 152-154) and pass them out. Explain to the group that in the next session we will be looking at neighbor and neighborhood winners and losers under economic globalization. We will be dividing into several small groups that represent three different imaginary local realities of economic globalization. List the three scenarios posted on newsprint and ask group members to think about which group they would want to be a part of. In addition to reviewing Chapter 3 in the text, ask them to think about the particular identities in the scenarios. Who are the winners or losers? Tell them to review the material and make notes.

Encourage the group to look for statements of ecumenical or policy groups concerning principles of globalization. The more contributions come from members of the group, the richer your group's experience is likely to be.

Session 3

In this session we consider some of the connections that economic globalization creates between communities and individuals in different parts of the world, connections that are described in Chapter 3. Participants will discuss what is at stake in these connections and consider alternative ways in which relationships between communities and nations might be organized. They will think about the human rights that are involved and the ethical choices that individuals and communities need to consider as we work toward a just global economy for all.

In any discussion of globalization the word competition comes up frequently. Companies lay off workers in order to be more competitive. Workers are told to work harder and faster in order to be more competitive. Corporations move their production to countries where labor costs are lower in order to be more competitive. We will examine this key value of globalization to see how it stands up to our faith imperatives. Is competition the economic strategy that will build global community?

Goals:

- To explore the meaning of competition as an economic value in the lives of real people in real communities.

- To explore choices for alternate economic values to build livelihoods for all.

Materials and Supplies:

- copies of group process and questions
- copies of "Globalization Reality" scenarios
- copies of "Globalization Interconnections—Livelihoods" chart (Appendix, p. 156)
- identity cards for neighbor-to-neighbor dialogues
- newsprint with group process and questions
- group statements on newsprint
- *India & Pakistan* by Glory Dharmaraj
- copy of the article "The Best Job in Town," by Katherine Boo from *The New Yorker,* July 5, 2004 (www.newyorker.com)
- symbols about work or workers for Worship Center

Preparation:

- Make copies of both the process each group should follow and the overall questions that they will need to answer so that each member of the group can make their own notes and have their own record of the discussion (see "Neighbor-to-Neighbor Dialogues," Appendix, p. 155).

- Each member of the group will also need to have a copy of the "Globalization Reality" scenarios (Appendix, pp. 152-154) and "Globalization Interconnections—Livelihoods" chart (Appendix, p. 156) for note taking for their group. While these may have been given out at the end of the previous session, have extra copies available for this session.

- Prepare identity cards for the potential players in each of the neighbor-to-neighbor dialogues, or have blank cards to hand out to each group so they can make their own identity cards. It is a way to help the groups identify the various players that are present in each local reality.

- On newsprint, print the questions that make up the process for the groups, as well as the two questions that make up their task, and post where they can be easily read.

- Post any general conference or ecumenical group statements of principles that may be helpful (see Chapter 3). Also print and post similar statements from faith perspectives from other sources, and provide space for participants to print and post statements from their own research.

- Create three distinct spaces for small group work, preferably three tables where groups can talk together without being overheard by others. If you have more than one room available or another group could meet in the space close by, this is ideal.

- You will need a copy of *India & Pakistan* by Glory Dharmaraj and the article from *The New Yorker* magazine.

- Add symbols about work and workers to enhance your worship center. Or ask members if they have symbols of their own work that they would want to place in the worship center.

Opening Activities

1. Opening Prayer (5 minutes)

Open the session with prayer, or invite a participant to do so.

2. Bible Study (10 minutes)

In this Bible study the group will brainstorm ethical principles that grow out of the Good Samaritan text that might be applied to the economic realities of the connection between people and nations.

Ask one member of the group to slowly read the story of the Good Samaritan in Luke 10. Then ask the group to name some of the ethical principles that seem to be operating in the story of the Good Samaritan; for example, sharing with others, creating an ongoing response to a problem, recognizing robbery, mutual responsibility for the well being of others, and redistribution of wealth. Record each suggestion on newsprint. Suggest that participants keep these principles in mind to see whether any of the individual solutions that appear in the story give guidance about responses to collective economic problems.

Learning Activities

3. Neighbor-to-Neighbor Dialogues (45 minutes)

Explain to the group that this activity will be a chance to imagine the kind of neighbor-to-neighbor cross-border conversations that need to take place in order to build just connections between workers in one community and workers in another community, consumers in one community and consumers in another community, and so forth. Remind them that cross-border conversations are profiled in Chapter 3. As they learned at the end of the last lesson, for this activity the group will be divided into three smaller groups:

- **Group 1:** a group considering the possibility of the placement of a Wal-Mart store in their community;

- **Group 2:** a community and a group of workers employed in a high-tech industry who faces downsizing as the company moves to hire technical workers in the Third World;

- **Group 3:** residents of a rural community that has recently experienced an influx of immigrant workers.

The groups have three tasks:

1. To make suggestions on how to change this situation in order to promote the well-being of all;

2. To highlight the process of change and to help each other to move through it;

3. To identify what might be some of the trade-offs and sacrifices that will need to be made.

Each group will follow a process for their discussion. Stress to participants that there are no perfect or magic solutions; that it is expected that each solution will have its positive and negative points; that compromises will need to be made.

Questions for Group Reflections

- **What are the human rights involved in this situation? What are the differences in the capabilities to achieve those rights?** (*Suggest that they refer to the discussion of rights and capabilities in Chapters 1–3.*)

- **What agreement is there within the group on goals? Are there global commons about livelihoods that include individuals and communities in all countries?**

- **Who makes the decisions in this situation?**

- **Who pays the costs and who reaps the benefits?** (*Refer to notes made on the "Globalization Interconnections Worksheet" in Chapter 3.*)

Each group will hold a discussion on these issues with participation of all the key persons who might be involved. It might be helpful to hand out the identity cards that have the names of potential participants on them, assigning roles to different members of each group; or the blanks you have on hand, so the group make that choice themselves. Have additional cards available for any other actors that the group decides are important to have in their conversation.

It is very important that the groups understand that the purpose of this exercise is discussion and dialogue; it should *never* be a debate between two sides. The relationships between those in the discussion are not to be understood as adversarial, but as persons coming from different perspectives trying to find a common solution.

After completing their discussions, groups will print (in brief phrases on newsprint) and post around the room:

- their suggestions for the changes that they would like to see and any actions that they think they can take to support one another;

- the trade-offs and sacrifices. Perhaps the major solution could take the form of a newspaper headline.

During the break all members of the group will have a chance to go around the room and read the results of the three discussions.

During these discussions, circulate among the three groups, stopping to listen for a while to each discussion and to also be available to any of the groups for questions that they may have. It is important that you be able to absorb the basic flow of the conversation of all the groups. This will enable you to sense where groups may be having difficulty or where the discussion is moving off base, so that you can try to put it back on track.

Globalization Reality #1: The Coming of Wal-Mart

Averagetown, U.S.A. is one of a cluster of communities with populations of 50,000 or less in a mixed agricultural and industrial part of a moderate sized state. Wal-Mart has approached the Town Council with a proposal to build a store within the town limits. The new store will employ one to 150 persons at minimum wage, but about 10 percent of the jobs will be managerial positions, some of which will be recruited locally. The store will offer a wide variety of products and services. A number of small businesses in the area—hardware stores, small dress shops, and so forth, will be in competition with the new Wal-Mart store.

Having heard about controversies surrounding Wal-Mart stores in other communities, a group of local citizens and members of the Town Council propose opening a conversation with workers in China because these workers produce a majority of the goods that are sold at the Wal-Mart store. The goal of these conversations is to try to understand some of the impacts for their community, and for workers in China, of the opening of the Wal-Mart store.

Participants in the conversation:

- Potential Wal-Mart consumers
- Wal-Mart workers from other stores
- Chinese workers
- Local small-business owners
- U.S. producers of other products sold at Wal-Mart
- Elected officials from the community

Resources for the discussion:

- "China and Globalization" from the text in Chapter 2 (p. 35)
- General Conference statements

Globalization Reality #2: Crises for Skilled University Trained Workers

Radiology Associates is a company that provides MRI (magnetic resonance imaging) reading services for physicians and hospitals. Because of Internet technologies, a company is able to provide services for physicians and hospitals not only within their own community, but also within a wide geographical area. Radiology Associates is located close to several universities and has been able to draw on a large pool of university graduates for its work force. Its employees receive competitive salaries and generous benefits. However, the Board of Directors has made several trips to India recently and has concluded that they can be more "competitive" if they use an equally qualified work force in India for one quarter of the costs of employing U.S. workers. The company is therefore proposing to downsize its U.S.-based work force and shift most of its work to India. Town officials and employees decide to make their own visit to India to discuss this situation with their counterparts.

Participants in the conversation:

• Technology workers

• Company management

• Patients who need MRIs

• Indian technology workers

• Town officials

Resources for the discussion:

• Chapter 3 on outsourcing and Indian workers

• *India & Pakistan* mission study by Glory Dharmaraj, Chapter 6, pp.115-117

• Copies of *The New Yorker* magazine article on India (www.newyorker.com)

• Their own global connection worksheets prepared during study of Chapter 3

• Newspaper and magazine articles on outsourcing to India

Globalization Reality #3: Local Communities, Immigrant Workers, and Jobs

Small town U.S.A. is a rural community in the South with less than 40,000 residents. The community has recently seen a migration of Mexican and Central American immigrants to the community. The community has one factory that produces women's apparel for one of the major women's international manufacturing firms on a subcontracted basis. Although the factory has had its ups and downs, over the years it has provided employment for some town residents. Now increasing numbers of immigrant women are employed in the factory, replacing locally born residents as they retire or move to larger communities in search of better job opportunities. The longtime residents and new immigrant residents of the community remain separated and there is some sentiment being publicly expressed about the immigrants "taking our jobs."

A group of concerned citizens, including a United Methodist Women's local unit in the church that has tried to reach out to new immigrants by creating a multicultural service, decides to convene a conversation in the community on the issue of jobs.

Participants in the conversation:

• Factory workers: longtime residents and immigrants

• UMW local unit members

• Visiting family members of the immigrant workers

• Town elected officials

Resources for the discussion:

• Chapter 3 on immigrants and migration

• "Globalization Interconnections" worksheet

• "Negotiating the Global Commons: Livelihoods" worksheet

Break (10 minutes)

4. Debriefing and Discussion (35 minutes)

After each group has completed its work and posted its conclusions, ask group members to volunteer some of the things that they learned from this exercise. Record all of their observations on newsprint. Once the list is complete, ask the group to consider which of these learnings are most important in determining an approach to how to work on issues of economic globalization. Have them vote by raising their hands so that the most important ones can be identified. Then have a general discussion to deepen the understanding around some of these points.

ASK:

• What were some points in common across the three groups?

• Are there some principles that we believe are important from our perspective for building a just global economy?

• Did the exercise give us any new perspective on the idea of "U.S. jobs?"

Worship: Restoring the Breach (10 minutes)

The purpose of this worship service is to prayerfully consider that all-important task of crossing borders, going beyond our own reality, and building bridges to other realities in order to work for justice.

Call to Worship

Leader: Come, let us worship our God, our continual guide, who satisfies our needs and makes our bodies strong.

People: Come, let us worship our God, who is rebuilding the ancient ruins and raising up the foundations for many generations.

All: Come, let us listen to our God so that we can be repairers of the breach between neighbors and restorers of neighborhoods.

—Adapted from Isaiah 58

Intercession: Lighting the Candles of Struggle and Celebration

All: Celebrating that God has placed us in a world where we are connected to all life and recognizing that we need to take responsibility for ensuring that justice is the foundation of these relationships; we offer our prayers to God on behalf of the global reality of neighbor and neighborhood.

Representatives of each of the three groups are invited to come forward and light a candle recalling some of the struggles in difficult places in having conversations about these relationships. When all who wish to have spoken, the response by the group is:

All: We light these lights and offer these prayers for the ongoing struggle to build equity and justice for and between all workers and communities.

Representatives of the three groups are invited to come and share concerns from their discussion that celebrate some of the opportunities that dialogue across borders makes possible. When all who wish to have spoken, the response of the group is:

All: We light these candles to celebrate and praise God for the exciting opportunities to build justice that God has given us through dialogue across borders and boundaries.

Invite any other prayers and concerns to be raised.

All: Amen.

Suggested Hymns

"For the Healing of the Nations" (*United Methodist Hymnal*, #428; consider using the alternative tune, "God the Sculptor of the Mountains," in *The Faith We Sing*, #2060); "Jesu, Jesu" (*United Methodist Hymnal*, #432); "For the Troubles and the Sufferings" (*Global Praise 3*, #162); "Pray for Peace" (*Global Praise 2*, #58).

Closing Prayer

Ask participants to reflect silently on what it would take to restore God's shalom to the world in terms of the global economy. Then close with a prayer of your own.

Assignments: (5 minutes)

Ask the class to read Chapter 4. They should review in particular the "Global Media Communications Conglomerates," (p. 81) "Cyberlords," (p. 83) and "Ultra Concentrated Media" (p. 133) charts and think about where these media giants are a part of their lives. Ask them to make notes for the "Negotiating the Global Commons: Communications" worksheet and bring it to the session.

Also ask the class to think seriously about how globalization affects people in their own community and how it affects them personally. Ask them to read Chapter 5 and to review the materials and notes that they have developed over the course of the study. Tell them to bring materials for the lessons with them to class as resources for their final discussions, particularly the Global Commons and the Globalization Interactions worksheets. Review the materials on the Good Samaritan and the General Conference Statements, and those of other religious groups. Ask the group to recall some of the activities described that are working issues of globalization, and think about which ones might be useful in their own communities.

Session 4

Understanding Globalization, Global Media, and Building Global Commons

Global media, information, and communications technologies bring the realities of economic globalization into our homes. They're both medium and message. Much has been said about their power to transform our lives. But not enough has been said about how media and information project a world of plenty that is enjoyed by some while cruelly reminding others of their distance from that world. In this session we will put ourselves in the global media and information technology picture; to think about our values and our vision for having local communities derive positive benefits from global media and information technologies. It is fitting that we begin our envisioning of new possibilities in this age of globalization by thinking about how we can use these all powerful tools of communications to play a key role in building and preserving a global commons where all the neighborhood has the capability for living an abundant life.

Goals

- To show how global media, information, and communications technologies touch our lives and how we can use them to help shape a just future for all.

- To map the broad outlines of our vision of the global commons and its biblical and theological underpinnings.

- To outline some personal and collective areas for action: challenging economic globalization and building global community.

Materials and Supplies:

- newsprint for each group to record its findings

- copies of "Cyberlords," "Negotiating the Global Commons: Communications," and "Globalization Interconnections—Global Media" worksheets for each participant for note taking.

- prepared newsprint sheets (see Preparation) and sheets from past sessions

- materials for the Worship Center (see Preparation)

- 2" x 2" self-stick notes in two different colors and strips of colored paper

- Bibles

- hymnals

Preparation:

- Arrange the room for maximum flexibility and easy movement in order to accommodate the mix of whole-group and small-group activities that are included in this lesson.

- Article 19 of the Universal Declaration of Human Rights should be printed out on large paper and posted in the front of the room during Activity 3. Also have on hand materials and charts from Chapter 4 in the text and from previous sessions that may be useful reference material for group activities.

- For the 24-hour clock exercise, copy the clock illustration (Appendix, p. 157). Post this sheet in the front of the room.

- Make copies of the "Cyberlords" sheet (p. 83) for each member of your class.

- Make copies of "Globalization Interconnections—Global Media" (Appendix, p. 159), Article 19 of the Universal Declaration of Human Rights (Appendix, p. 158), and "Cloud of Witnesses" (Appendix, p. 158) for each participant and copies of "Negotiating the Global Commons: Communications" worksheets for each group.

- Place symbols of previous sessions in the Worship Center. Also add materials that symbolize global media and information technologies, like a palm pilot, cell phone, radio, or the like. Be sure to have on hand enough candles for the group contributions to the intercessory prayer.

- Have plenty of newsprint and markers on hand for each group.

- If they are not already posted, put up the newsprint statements from previous sessions.

- Have a good supply of 2" x 2" self-stick notes in two different colors available as a way to identify priorities. You'll also need a supply of colored paper that can be torn into strips and used to write down commitments. These will be placed upon the altar during the closing worship.

Opening Activity

1. 24-hour Clock: Creating a Picture of Global Media and Information Technologies In Our Lives (10 minutes)

Ask each person to think about the times during their day, beginning when they wake up, that global media and information technologies—radios, TVs, the Internet, and so forth—are part of their lives.

Record on the large newsprint clock the number of contacts for all members of the group. If your group has both men and women, you may wish to record separate totals for men and women in order to see if any gender differences will be revealed. Now record the kind of media that was involved. Was it a local station or a network station or syndicated program? Was it an independent station? Finally, ask what information is available about the ownership patterns from this exercise and record that information as well.

Learning Activities

2. The Global Media Giants and Us (5 minutes)

Hand out the copies of the "**Ultra Concentrated Media**" sheet that you print from www.mediachannel.org/ownership/moguls-printable-150dpi.pdf and ask each person to take five minutes to look over the sheet and underline or circle every company to which they have listened, from which they bought something, or with which they have had contact. (You may want to enlarge the chart when you make copies.)

After the entire group has finished marking their sheets, take a few minutes to ask and record their reactions to this exercise.

Ultra Concentrated Media Chart

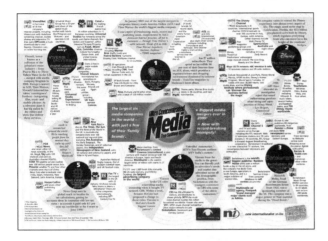

This chart can be viewed on screen or printed in color from **www.mediachannel.org/ ownership/moguls-printable-150dpi.pdf**

After the entire group has finished marking their sheets, take a few minutes to ask and record their reactions to this exercise.

ASK:

• Were you surprised by what you discovered?

• Were you surprised by the interconnections of the media companies?

3. Envisioning a Local Commons for Information (15 minutes)

Pass out the blank "Negotiating the Global Commons" worksheets and ask class members to review any of their notes from reading this chapter. Call participants' attention to the posted newsprint sheet with Article 19 of the Universal Declaration of Human Rights. Divide the group into smaller groups and ask them to develop a list of the important things that will be necessary in order to achieve the right to communicate for all at the local level.

They may wish to consider some of the following questions to help them develop their list:

1. Where do we see these rights exercised locally?

2. Are their voices missing from local media?

3. What does our media teach us about the rest of the world?

4. How does media conglomerate ownership affect the right to communicate at the local level?

5. What is needed to enhance the right to communicate locally? What might community cable access do? How could community controlled broadband Internet access help to bridge the digital divides?

6. What training is needed?

Once the groups have finished ask them to post their ideas on newsprint sheets around the walls of the room. Invite them to walk around the room to look at ideas from all the groups. Encourage them to take a break as necessary during this time.

4. Articulating Our Biblical and Theological Mandate (20 minutes)

Tell the group that in this final session, it is time to summarize what has been learned and make some plans for making a difference. Ask each group to review the biblical/theological statements presented during the study and displayed on newsprint around the room: Bible study, General Conference statements, ecumenical statements, and so forth, as well as the "Cloud of Witnesses" handout that includes some excerpts about economic globalization from ecumenical statements from around the world. Invite the groups to develop a brief three-sentence statement that expresses why Christians must care about economic globalization. This is a statement of faith rather than articulation of issues. Ask groups to record completed statements on newsprint and post on the walls.

5. Gallery Walk (5 minutes)

Once all the statements have been posted give the class five minutes to walk around and read all of the statements.

6. Broad Outlines for the Global Commons (20 minutes)

The "Negotiating the Global Commons: Communications" worksheets that have been created during the course of the study will be the basic resource for this activity. An additional resource should be the personal journaling notes on the common good, rights, and capabilities.

Ask each group to reflect on their faith statements and the worksheets in order to develop a priority list of the global commons. This list might be expressed in terms of rights and capabilities. Stress that it is not necessary to list everything they have talked about, but to try and select those things that they think are most important for building global community. The list should then be completed and posted on the wall alongside the group's statement of faith.

7. Gallery Walk (5 minutes)

Explain that the next two exercises will be about making action plans and commitments to work on issues related to economic globalization. In order to determine groups for the final exercise, give each person one of each of two different colors of 2" x 2" self-stick notes. Designate one color note for first priority and the other color for second priority. Tell them to put their name or initials clearly on each note. As they walk around the room and view all of the results of group discussions, ask them to place the sticky notes by their first and second priorities for action by Christians at the local level.

8. Local Action Strategies for Christians (20 minutes)

Using the priorities identified from the self-stick notes, divide the group into small groups based on major areas of interest. The task of each group is to formulate some specific group action strategies for working on the problems of economic globalization that were identified. For example, a United Methodist Women local unit might decide on actions that would reach out to women in the community who might be directly affected by globalization, such as immigrant women or women in a particular industry. Or a local congregation might try to organize ecumenical or interfaith services that would address the issues of globalization from a variety of faith traditions. The goal is to make the action strategies as practical as possible based on the capacity and sphere of influence of the different groups within the church.

Have groups record the results of their discussion on newsprint. Ask that they include a one-sentence overall goal and then three major actions to be taken. Request that the group write the proposed actions on slips of the colored paper. These will be a part of their contribution to the closing worship service. If you have the capacity you might want to transfer all of the information from these exercises into the computer and send it out to all the members of the class after the course is finished.

Closing Worship of Commitment (20 minutes)

The closing worship service is to voice and celebrate commitments to work on issues of economic globalization. Hand out two additional strips of colored paper to each participant. Allow a few minutes for participants to write down one commitment that they would like to make as individuals toward challenging economic globalization and building global community. Suggest that they write the commitments out twice. One paper is for them to keep and the other will be placed on the altar during the final worship.

Call to Worship

Leader: Holy God, we gather before you this day as your people who have been on a journey of learning.

People: **You have opened our hearts and minds to recognize the signs of your transforming power at work in our world.**

Leader: That power which continues to feed the hungry, clothe the naked, free the oppressed and break every yoke.

People: **We have heard the voices of others who live in the midst of globalization, and you have shown us our need for repentance because of our own complicity in systems of domination and injustice.**

All: **Fill us with your Holy Spirit, Teacher God. As a covenant community, help us to recommit ourselves to working for a global economic order that manifests an economy of life.**

Suggested Hymns

"Oh, For a Thousand Tongues to Sing" *(United Methodist Hymnal,* #57); "Make Me a Channel of Your Peace" *(The Faith We Sing,* #2171); "Rise Up, All You Nations" *(Global Praise 3,* #9)

Scripture

1 John 3:11-18 or Luke 10:25-37: the story of the Good Samaritan

Litany of the Economy of Life

Leader: Let us become, by God's grace, the faithful communion of saints that proclaims the gospel of love and justice and jubilee for the whole earth.

People: **The sacred gift of life that is the free gift of God's grace is for all and for all time.**

Leader: Who has the right to participate in the economy and society?

People: **God's gifts are for the use of all to live.**

Leader: Can everything and everyone's labor be owned and traded for a price in the market?

People: **Earth and all life have their origins in God and belong to God. They cannot be commodified.**

Leader: Can we live in an economy that promotes survival of the fittest and cares not for survival of the weak?

People: **The Biblical vision is for the care of the poor and the vulnerable.**

Leader: Can we accept discrimination and exclusion and unequal distribution of wealth and power?

People: **These things violate the commandment to love God and neighbor.**

Leader: How do we understand the fullness of life offered by Jesus?

People: **It is having food, clothing, work, and health; but also belonging and caring, self-realization, and experiencing and celebrating community.**

All: We practice an economy of life—an economy of solidarity and sharing. God's economy is an economy of the whole earth community.

Time of Intercession: Lighting of the Candles of Hope and Commitment

Leader: Knowing that all is in the hands of God, we come now to place our hopes and our commitments before God and before each other. Let us pray.

All: We light these candles to recall those who suffer and struggle because powerful economic forces care more for profits and acquiring wealth than they do for the health and well-being of families and communities. We celebrate the breaking through of God's justice, building a future whose foundation is solidarity, equality, and mutual respect.

Individual members of the group are invited to come forward and light a candle, placing a commitment paper on the altar. They can share their commitment or present it silently. One representative from each of the groups comes to present the action goal agreed to by the group. The group may wish to hum softly "This Little Light of Mine," while the commitments are being made.

All: We offer these lights as evidence of our commitment to global community built on love and justice. We light these candles to celebrate the connectedness that globalization brings to our world and God's economy of life.

Suggested Hymns

"Here I Am, Lord" (*United Methodist Hymnal*, #593); "With Passion in Our Hearts" (*Global Praise 2*, #122); "They'll Know We Are Christians By Our Love" (*The Faith We Sing*, #2223); "Sent Out in Jesus' Name" (*Global Praise 2*, #113)

Benediction

We go into the world because God is working there, Christ is suffering there, and the Spirit is caring for life and is resisting destructive principalities and powers. We go to love the neighbor. Amen.

—Adapted from Alternative Globalization Addressing Peoples and Earth (AGAPE), WCC, Geneva, 2005.

Sources

Used to Prepare Chapters and Study Guide

Introduction

General Conference Resolution 206. "Economic Justice for a New Millennium." *The Book of Resolutions.* Nashville: The United Methodist Publishing House, 2004.

General Conference Resolution 208. "Pathways to Economic Justice." *The Book of Resolutions.* Nashville: The United Methodist Publishing House, 2004.

Chapter 1

Circle of Rights—Economic, Social and Cultural Rights Activism: A Training Resource. Washington, DC: International Human Rights Internship Program and Asian Forum for Human Rights and Development, 2000.

Economics Education: Building a Movement for Global Economic Justice. Chicago: The Praxis/Economic Justice Project, American Friends Service Committee, 2001.

Ellwood, Wayne and John McMurty. *The No-Nonsense Guide to Globalization.* No-Nonsense Guides, New York: New Internationalist Publications, Ltd., 2002. www.newint.org/shop/us/nonoglob.htm.

General Conference Resolution 206. "Economic Justice for a New Millennium." *The Book of Resolutions.* Nashville: The United Methodist Publishing House, 2004.

General Conference Resolution 208. "Pathways to Economic Justice." *The Book of Resolutions.* Nashville: The United Methodist Publishing House, 2004.

General Conference Resolution 361. "Privatization." *The Book of Resolutions.* Nashville: The United Methodist Publishing House, 2004.

"Globalization." Policy Reference Committee II Report, Appendix II. Eighth Assembly. Geneva: World Council of Churches, 1998. http://www.wcc-coe.org/wcc/assembly/or-8d-e.html.

Hahnel, Robin. *Panic Rules!: Everything You Need to Know About the Global Economy.* Cambridge, Massachusetts: South End Press, 1999.

Social Principles ¶ 160. I. "The Natural World." *The Book of Resolutions.* Nashville: The United Methodist Publishing House, 2004.

Social Principles ¶ 165. VI. "The World Community." *The Book of Resolutions.* Nashville: The United Methodist Publishing House, 2004.

Sources (continued)

Chapter 2

Black, Maggie. *The No-Nonsense Guide to Water*. No-Nonsense Guides. New York: New Internationalist Publications, 2004. www.newint.org/shop/us/nonowater.htm.

"Bottled Up and Tapped Out: Why Bottled Water Purity is a Myth and Reliance on Bottled Water is a Threat." Washington, DC: Public Citizen, www.wateractivist.org.

Condon, Scott. "Aspen's Fiji Water Earns Honor from Colin Powell." *The Aspen Times*, October 29, 2004. http://www.aspentimes.com/article/20041029/NEWS/110290027&SearchID=7322295166695.

Defend the Global Commons newsletter. Water for All Campaign. Public Citizen. www.wateractivist.org.

Economics Education: Building a Movement for Global Economic Justice. The Praxis/Economic Justice Project, American Friends Service Committee, Chicago, 2001.

General Conference Resolution 13. "Protection of Water." *The Book of Resolutions*. Nashville: The United Methodist Publishing House, 2004.

Kidd, Ada. "Women and Water." *Response*. November 2004.

Klare, Michael T. *Resource Wars: The New Landscape of Global Conflict*. New York: Henry Holt and Co., 2002.

Nawaikula, Niko. "Land Rights in Fiji—A Sad Irony." Native Land Trust Board, 2002. http://www.nltb.com.fj/commentary/00_05_02.html.

Nazombe, elmira. Interview with Linda Schramm, Women's Division Director, General Board of Global Ministries, The United Methodist Church. New York, April 2005.

Nazombe, elmira. Telephone interview with Ada Kidd, August 29, 2005.

Nazombe, elmira. Telephone interview with Ann Whiting, *Michigan Christian Advocate*, July 12, 2005.

Nazombe, elmira. Telephone interview with Virisila Buadromo, Executive Director, Fiji Women's Rights Movement, April 9, 2005.

Ragogo, Matalita. "Fiji Water Making Waves: Pristine Taste and Savvy Marketing Are Driving Fiji's Biggest Export." *Pacific Magazine*, July 2003. http://www.pacificislands.cc/pm72003/pmdefault.php?urlarticleid=0014.

"Support of Water Protection/Boycott of Nestlé." West Michigan Annual Conference, United Methodist Church, Item 17, June 2004. www.westmichiganconference.org/ ac_petition_detail.asp?PKValue=17.

"Water—Every Drop Counts." *New Internationalist*, March 2003. www.newint.org/issue354/contents.htm.

"Who Owns Your Water?" Washington, DC: Public Citizen. www.wateractivist.org.

"Who's Taking Over" GATS Attack! Series. Polaris Institute, 2003. www.polarisinstitute.org/edu_tools/wto_manual/wto_man_index_PRINT.htm.

Chapter 3

Anderson, Sarah and John Cavanaugh with Thea Lee. *Field Guide to the Global Economy*. Institute for Policy Studies. New Press, 2000.

Balakrishnan, Radhika, ed. *The Hidden Assembly Line: Gender Dynamics of Subcontracted Work in a Global Economy*. Bloomfield, Connecticut: Kumarian Press, 2002.

Boo, Katherine. "The Best Job in Town: The Americanization of Chennai." *The New Yorker*, July 5, 2004. www.newyorker.com.

"China Has 1.85 Million Domain Names." *Chinascope*, April 16, 2005. www.chinascope.org/en.

Fishman, Ted C. "The Chinese Century." *The New York Times Magazine*. New York: July 4, 2004, p. 24.

Folbre, Nancy, coordinator and writer. *The Field Guide to the U.S. Economy*, The Center for Popular Economics. New York: Pantheon Books, 1989.

General Conference Resolution 199. "United Methodist Use of Fair Trade Coffee." *The Book of Resolutions*. Nashville: The United Methodist Publishing House, 2004.

General Conference Resolution 237. "Rights of Workers." *The Book of Resolutions*. Nashville: The United Methodist Publishing House, 2004.

General Conference Resolution 309. "Globalization and its Impact on Human Dignity and Human Rights." *The Book of Resolutions*. Nashville: The United Methodist Publishing House, 2004.

Global Exchange website. http://www.globalexchange.org.

"Growth-hungry McDonald's looking to expand in China." *Chinascope*, May 16, 2005. www.chinascope.org/en.

Sources (continued)

Henderson, Russ. Various articles. *Mobile Register*. http://nl.newsbank.com.

"How Could FTAA Affect You?" Peoples' Consultation on FTAA. www.peoplesconsultation.org.

"Is Wal-Mart Good for America?" PBS documentary, November 2004.

Louie, Miriam Ching Yoon. *Sweatshop Warriors: Immigrant Women Workers Take On the Global Factory*. Cambridge, Massachusetts: South End Press, 2001.

Make Trade Fair Campaign. Oxfam International. www.maketradefair.com.

"Microsoft to launch MSN China with Shanghai Alliance Investment." Chinascope, May 11, 2005. www.chinascope.org/en.

"Migration: 'A force of history.'" Factfile: Global Migration. BBC News. http://news.bbc.co.uk.

Naples, Nancy A. and Manisha Desai, eds. *Women's Activism and Globalization: Linking Local Struggles and Transnational Politics*. New York: Routledge Press, 2002.

Nazombe, elmira. Interview with Vera Moore, United Methodist Women. Mobile, Alabama, March, 2005.

Nazombe, elmira. Telephone interview with Deborah Long, Public Relations, Southern Shrimp Alliance, March 2005.

Nazombe, elmira. Telephone interview with Myra Sutton, United Methodist Women. Bayou La Batre, Alabama, April 2005.

Stalker, Peter. *The No-Nonsense Guide to International Migration*. No-Nonsense Guides. New York: New Internationalist Publications, 2001. www.newint.org/shop/us/nonointmig.htm.

"Starbucks Aims to Alter China's Taste in Caffeine." Chinascope, May 23, 2005. www.chinascope.org/en.

"Trading Away Our Rights: Women Working in Global Supply Chains." Make Trade Fair. Oxfam, 2004. http://publications.oxfam.org.uk/oxfam/display.asp?isbn=0855985232.

"Wal-Mart's Chinese suppliers shift base to India." Chinascope, May 23, 2005. www.chinascope.org/en.

Zerkel, Mary, ed. Economics Education: *Building a Movement for Global Economic Justice*. Chicago: The Praxis/Economic Justice Project, American Friends Service Committee, 2001.

Chapter 4

"The Big Ten." *The Nation*, January 7 and 14, 2002. http://thenation.com/special/bigten.html.

Consumer Voice for Communications Choice. http://www.hearusnow.org.

"Falling Through the Net: A Survey of the 'Have-Nots' in Rural and Urban America." National Telecommunications and Information Administration, July 1995. http://www.nita.doc.gov/ntiahome/fallingthru.html.

"The Fallout from the Telecommunications Act of 1996: Unintended Consequences and Lessons Learned." Common Cause, May 2005. http://www.commoncause.org.

General Conference Resolution 363. "Proper Use of Information and Communications Technologies." *The Book of Resolutions*. Nashville: The United Methodist Publishing House, 2004.

Global Communications for Justice: A National Council of Churches Policy Statement. National Council of Churches of Christ in the U.S.A. Approved by the General Board, November 11, 1993.

Herman, Edward S. and Robert W. McChesney. *The Global Media: The New Missionaries of Corporate Capitalism*. London: Cassell, 1997.

"Is KMEL The Peoples' Station? A Community Assessment of 106.1 KMEL." Youth Media Council, November 2002.

McChesney, Robert W. "The New Global Media: It's a Small World of Big Conglomerates." *The Nation*, November 29, 1999. http://www.thenation.com/doc/19991129/mcchesney.

Nazombe, elmira. Interview with Taishi Duchicela, Media Justice Coordinator, Youth Media Council. Oakland, California, May 2005.

Nazombe, elmira. Telephone interview with Julia Perkins, Media Staff, Coalition of Immokalee Workers. Immokalee, Florida, July 2005.

Nazombe, elmira. Telephone interviews with Nan Rubin, Community Media Services. New York, April 2005 and July 4, 2005.

Nazombe, elmira. Telephone interview with Rajeli Nicole, Executive Director, Isis International. Manilla, Philippines, May 2005.

Themba-Nixon, Makani. "Beyond the Digital Divide: A Brief Consideration of Emerging Economies, Technology, and Racial Justice." Applied Research Center, July 2000.

Themba-Nixon, Makani and Nan Rubin. "Speaking for Ourselves." *The Nation*. November 17, 2003. http://www.thenation.com/doc/20031117/thembanixon.

Sources (continued)

Chapter 5

Alternative Globalization Addressing Peoples and Earth (AGAPE): A Background Document.
Geneva: Justice, Peace, and Creation Team, World Council of Churches, 2003.

Taylor, Michael. *Christianity, Poverty and Wealth: The Findings of "Project 21."*
Geneva: World Council of Churches Publications, 2003.

Study Guide

Alternative Globalization Addressing Peoples and Earth (AGAPE): A Background Document.
Geneva: Justice, Peace, and Creation Team, World Council of Churches, 2003.

The Christian Principles of Communication. World Association for Christian Communication.
http://www.wacc.org.uk/wacc/content/pdf/100.

Taylor, Michael. *Christianity, Poverty and Wealth: The Findings of "Project 21."*
Geneva: World Council of Churches Publications, 2003.

Appendix

Investment:

Privatization:

Democratic Control:

Resources at Stake: Water, Food, etc.:

- **Jobs:**

- **Working Conditions—health and safety:**

- **Health care, Child care:**

- **Farmers and food:**

- **Intellectual property rights:**

    – Culture

    – Indigenous knowledge

    – Biodiversity

    – Access to essential medicines

- **Democratic Control:**

- **Monopoly control:**

- **Commercialized media culture:**

- **Public interest and voice:**

- **Access/connectivity:**

- **Uses and resources:**

FEDERAL COMMUNICATIONS COMMISSION RESPONSIBILITIES

- In charge of spectrum management

- Right technical and administrative regulations

- Administer policy goals set by Congress

- Distribute and review licenses to broadcast TV and radio

- Regulate cable industry, telephones, wireless communications, satellite broadcasting, and any device that may interfere with radio communications

- Auction the spectrum collecting usage fees for the treasury

- Study questions about fair policies governing emerging technologies

THE TELECOMMUNICATIONS ACT OF 1996

The promise: More competition, more jobs, more diversity, lower prices.

The provisions and consequences:

- Radio station ownership cap lifted—radio giants like Clear Channel created, substantial drop in minority-owned stations, homogenization of play lists, less local news.

- Expansion of limits on local TV station ownership raised to 35 percent of all viewers—increased media mergers and concentration, five companies control 75 percent of primetime viewing.

- Cable rates deregulated—rates increased by 50 percent between 1996 and 2003.

- Cable broadcast cross-ownership rules eased—90% of top cable stations and broadcast networks owned by the same networks.

- Digital cable license given to broadcasters—$70 billion of potential federal treasury revenue lost.

- Broadcast license term extended from five to eight years—broadcaster accountability to the public weakened.

- Universal service fund created—made funds available for community cable access.

- V-Chip requirements established—allows parents to control television programming for children.

206. Economic Justice for a New Millennium

V. Call to Action

The United Methodist Church, as a covenant of community committed to God's justice, must work toward a just global economy. Our Social Principles remind us that "in spite of general affluence in the industrialized nations, most of the persons in the world live in poverty. To provide basic needs such as food, clothing, shelter, education, health care, and other necessities, ways must be found to share more equitably the resources of the world" (¶ 163E). Faced with securing economic justice for a new millennium, the General Conference calls upon:

1. each local congregation and every central and annual conference to use this resolution and related resources as a foundation to initiate a study curriculum and social actions on global economic justice issues;

2. the whole church to work with people in local communities to identify specific economic issues that affect families, communities, and individuals, especially the impacts upon the lives of women. These issues include jobs with livable wages and benefits, debt, plant closings and relocation, public education, homelessness, affordable housing, and meeting sanitation, clean water, and energy needs. These issues should be addressed through the strategies of prayer, study, service, advocacy, community organizing, and economic development;

3. the General Board of Church and Society and the General Board of Global Ministries to engage in ongoing searches for and study of alternative and sustainable systems of economic order, shall work with local congregations, central and annual conferences to initiate and support legislative efforts at the local, state, national, and international levels that will address "Structures of Injustice" (Section III). Attention should be given to marginalized and indigenous people; the accountability or reform of transnational corporations and banks; personal and corporate investment responsibility; land reform, and the dependency of national economies on the military;

4. the general program agencies of the church and the General Board of Pension and Health Benefits to work with the Interfaith Center on Corporate Responsibility and support its *Principles for Global Corporate Responsibility;* and

5. all bodies of the church to be more intentional in using their investment portfolios to strengthen developing national economies and global economic justice. We also encourage central and annual conferences, local churches and individuals in wealthy nations to live a simpler, more modest lifestyle.

In order to be God's real community, we must realize that people are not here to serve an economic system, but economic systems must serve all people so all live in God's abundance.

ADOPTED 1988
REVISED AND ADOPTED 2000

208. Pathways to Economic Justice

Personal Pathways to Economic Justice

- Support locally based businesses.
- Recycle waste products and avoid use of disposable products where possible.
- Buy organic, locally produced foods as much as possible.
- Invest personal savings in stocks and mutual funds which are socially screened.
- Buy only clothing and other articles that you know are not manufactured by child labor, sweatshop, or slave labor.
- Engage in Bible study on economic justice.
- Take part in study groups on economic issues, using materials from groups like the People of Faith network.

Local Paths to Economic Justice

- Support local initiatives for moderate and low income housing.
- Support policies of Affirmative Action and Equal Opportunity employment.
- Open your church to house the homeless and feed the hungry.
- Each congregation commit a tithe (10 percent) of its budget to helping the poor and working for economic justice.
- Support full rights for farm workers, especially the right to organize and bargain collectively.

National and Global Paths to Economic Justice

- Conference United Methodist Women organizations take up at least one specific action project for economic justice in the next quadrennium.
- Make every annual conference staff racially and ethnically diverse at all levels.
- Support the right of governments to limit the international flow of capital.
- Deny Most Favored Nation Trade Status to nations which permit sweatshop, child, or slave labor, do not permit workers to organize, and do not guarantee workers a living wage by accepted international standards.
- Enact campaign finance reform that prevents corporations and special interest groups buying legislators and dominating the legislative process.
- Support public sector job creation to build highways, schools, and housing when the private sector is unable to provide jobs for all who need them.
- Support policies that encourage the use of renewable resources and limit the destruction of nonrenewable resources, leading to a sustainable environment.
- End the fiction that the corporation is a "person," a doctrine never envisioned by the founding fathers.
- Support Jubilee 2000 through living out its spirit and principles in the life of the community.

ADOPTED 2000

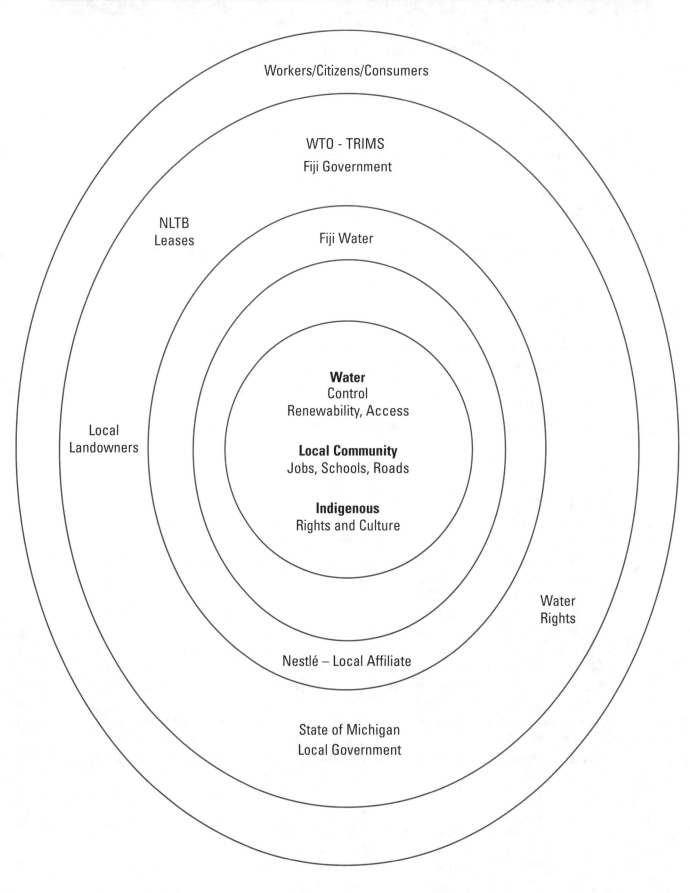

Workers/Citizens/Consumers

WTO - TRIMS
Fiji Government

NLTB
Leases

Fiji Water

Local
Landowners

Water
Control
Renewability, Access

Local Community
Jobs, Schools, Roads

Indigenous
Rights and Culture

Water
Rights

Nestlé – Local Affiliate

State of Michigan
Local Government

FORUM THEATRE

Forum Theatre is one of the methodologies developed by Augusto Boal and the Theatre of the Oppressed in Brazil. The Theatre of the Oppressed was developed as a way to help local communities use theatre to understand their own problems and develop and try out their own solutions. This methodology uses drama improvisation to consider alternatives for social change action. In this exercise a protagonist(s) tries to pose a solution to a particular problem. The action of the exercise is trying out alternative solutions until the group feels that a solution has been discovered that actually makes social change.

Steps:

1. Break into small groups. Each group creates a short improvisation that demonstrates a particular problem and portrays one person or group of persons (protagonists) who attempt to solve the problem. One person in the group agrees to play the role of the JOKER, whose task is to facilitate the action of the group.

2. A group then presents its improvisation. The improvisation should be repeated, but this time the audience can stop the performance at any time by yelling "STOP."

3. Whoever yells stop has to be prepared to replace the protagonist in the improvisation. The JOKER asks the group if the action proposed by the original protagonist actually changed the situation.

4. The improvisation is then performed by the new protagonist(s) trying out a new solution with all the other players maintaining their roles. The process can be repeated for as long as the group has new ideas about how to solve the problem.

5. Conclude the exercise by a discussion of the best solution and ways in which that solution might be implemented.

Tip: The role of the Joker is critical in keeping the action of the group flowing. The Joker needs to be assertive in getting the group to push hard to solutions that actually solve the problem as presented.

Race, Class, and Gender Analysis: This methodology can be very helpful in order to bring out the ways in which race, class, and gender identities affect problems and potential solutions.

Adapted from material developed by Carol Barton, June 2004.

The Coming of Wal-Mart

Averagetown, U.S.A. is one of a cluster of communities with populations of 50,000 or less in a mixed agricultural and industrial part of a moderate sized state. Wal-Mart has approached the Town Council with a proposal to build a store within the town limits. The new store will employ one to 150 persons at minimum wage, but about 10 percent of the jobs will be managerial positions, some of which will be recruited locally. The store will offer a wide variety of products and services. A number of small businesses in the area—hardware stores, small dress shops, and so forth, will be in competition with the new Wal-Mart store.

Having heard about controversies surrounding Wal-Mart stores in other communities, a group of local citizens and members of the Town Council propose opening a conversation with workers in China because these workers produce a majority of the goods that are sold at the Wal-Mart store. The goal of these conversations is to try to understand some of the impacts for their community, and for workers in China, of the opening of the Wal-Mart store.

Participants in the conversation:

- Potential Wal-Mart consumers
- Wal-Mart workers from other stores
- Chinese workers
- Local small-business owners
- U.S. producers of other products sold at Wal-Mart
- Elected officials from the community

Resources for the discussion:

- "China and Globalization" from the text in Chapter 2 (p. 35)
- General Conference statements

Crises for Skilled University Trained Workers

Radiology Associates is a company that provides MRI (magnetic resonance imaging) reading services for physicians and hospitals. Because of Internet technologies, a company is able to provide services for physicians and hospitals not only within their own community, but also within a wide geographical area. Radiology Associates is located close to several universities and has been able to draw on a large pool of university graduates for its work force. Its employees receive competitive salaries and generous benefits. However, the Board of Directors has made several trips to India recently and has concluded that they can be more "competitive" if they use an equally qualified work force in India for one quarter of the costs of employing U.S. workers. The company is therefore proposing to downsize its U.S.-based work force and shift most of its work to India. Town officials and employees decide to make their own visit to India to discuss this situation with their counterparts.

Participants in the conversation:

- Technology workers
- Company management
- Patients who need MRIs
- Indian technology workers
- Town officials

Resources for the discussion:

- Chapter 3 on outsourcing and Indian workers
- *India & Pakistan* mission study by Glory Dharmaraj, Chapter 6, pp. 115-117
- Copies of *The New Yorker* magazine July 5, article, "The Best Job in Town," on India (www.newyorker.com)
- Global connection worksheets prepared during study of Chapter 3
- Newspaper and magazine articles on outsourcing to India

Local Communities, Immigrant Workers, and Jobs

Small town U.S.A. is a rural community in the South with less than 40,000 residents. The community has recently seen a migration of Mexican and Central American immigrants to the community. The community has one factory that produces women's apparel for one of the major women's international manufacturing firms on a subcontracted basis. Although the factory has had its ups and downs, over the years it has provided employment for some town residents. Now increasing numbers of immigrant women are employed in the factory, replacing locally born residents as they retire or move to larger communities in search of better job opportunities. The longtime residents and new immigrant residents of the community remain separated and there is some sentiment being publicly expressed about the immigrants "taking our jobs."

A group of concerned citizens, including a United Methodist Women's local unit in the church that has tried to reach out to new immigrants by creating a multicultural service, decides to convene a conversation in the community on the issue of jobs.

Participants in the conversation:

- Factory workers: longtime residents and immigrants
- UMW local unit members
- Visiting family members of the immigrant workers
- Town elected officials

Resources for the discussion:

- Chapter 3 on immigrants and migration
- "Globalization Interconnections" worksheet
- "Negotiating the Global Commons: Livelihoods" worksheet

NEIGHBOR-TO-NEIGHBOR DIALOGUES

For this activity the group will be divided into three smaller groups:

Group 1: a group considering the possibility of the placement of a Wal-Mart store in their community;

Group 2: a community and a group of workers employed in a high-tech industry who faces downsizing as the company moves to hire technical workers in the Third World;

Group 3: residents of a rural community that has recently experienced an influx of immigrant workers.

The groups have three tasks:

1. To make suggestions on how to change this situation in order to promote the well-being of all;

2. To highlight the process of change and to help each other to move through it;

3. To identify what might be some of the trade-offs and sacrifices that will need to be made.

Each group will follow a process for their discussion. There are no perfect or magic solutions, that it is expected that each solution will have its positive and negative points, that compromises will need to be made.

Questions for Group Reflections

- **What are the human rights involved in this situation? What are the differences in the capabilities to achieve those rights?** (*Refer to the discussion of rights and capabilities in Chapters 1–3.*)

- **What agreement is there within the group on goals? Are there global commons about livelihoods that include individuals and communities in all countries?**

- **Who makes the decisions in this situation?**

- **Who pays the costs and who reaps the benefits?** (*Refer to notes made on the "Globalization Interconnections Worksheet" in Chapter 3.*)

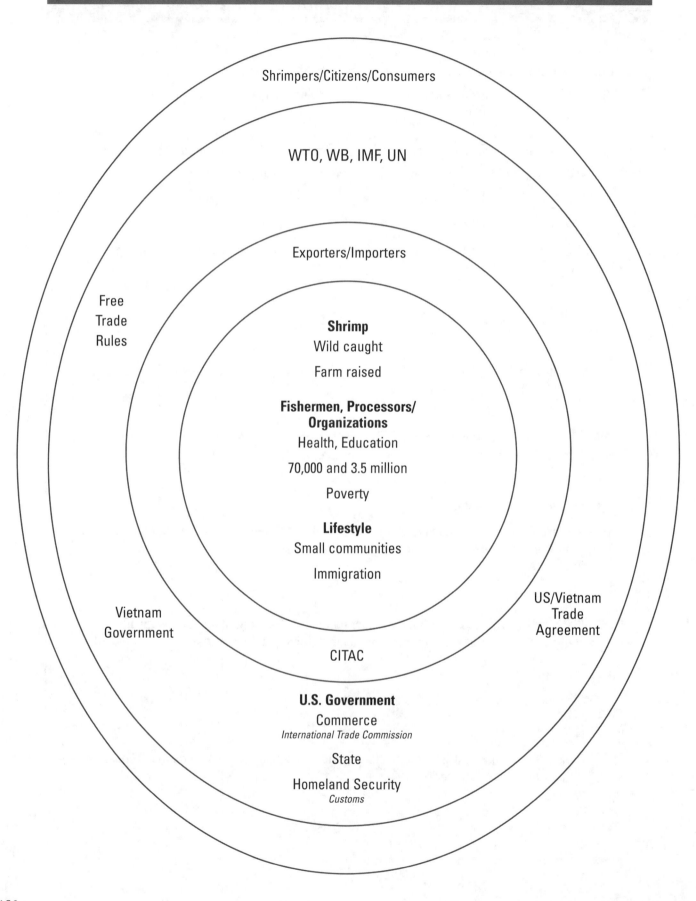

Shrimpers/Citizens/Consumers

WTO, WB, IMF, UN

Exporters/Importers

Free
Trade
Rules

Shrimp
Wild caught
Farm raised

**Fishermen, Processors/
Organizations**
Health, Education
70,000 and 3.5 million
Poverty

Lifestyle
Small communities
Immigration

US/Vietnam
Trade
Agreement

Vietnam
Government

CITAC

U.S. Government
Commerce
International Trade Commission
State
Homeland Security
Customs

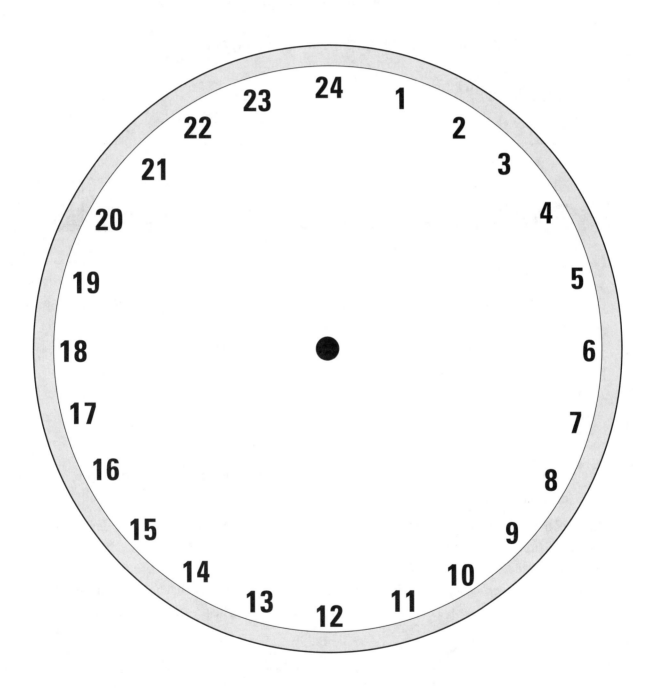

THE UNIVERSAL DECLARATION OF HUMAN RIGHTS, ARTICLE 19

"Everyone has a right to freedom of opinion and expression; this right includes freedom to hold opinions without interference and to seek, receive and impart information and ideas through any media and regardless of frontiers."

CLOUD OF WITNESSES ON GLOBALIZATION

WCC Assembly, 1998:

"The vision behind globalization includes a competing vision to the Christian commitment to the oikoumene, the unity of humankind and the whole inhabited earth," the assembly said, and recommended that "the logic of globalization needs to be challenged by an alternative way of life of community in diversity. Christians and churches should reflect on the challenge of globalization from a faith perspective and therefore resist the unilateral domination of economic and cultural globalization."

The ecumenical team at the UN World Summit for Social Development, Copenhagen, 1995 (or Geneva, 2000):

"Now is the time for people, their governments and the United Nations to claim a clear Jubilee vision and move boldly towards it, a vision of a global community whose interdependence is not reduced to trade and markets. This requires a change of heart, which recognizes that real value cannot be expressed in monetary terms, and that life in its many forms cannot be commodified. The economy should serve the well-being of people, rather than people being servants of the economy."

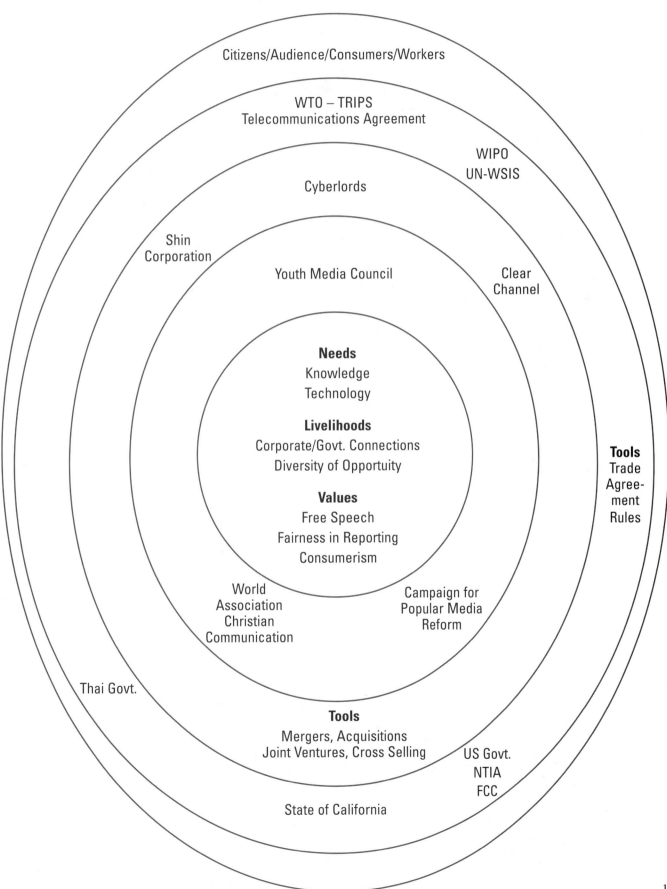

Citizens/Audience/Consumers/Workers

WTO – TRIPS
Telecommunications Agreement

WIPO
UN-WSIS

Cyberlords

Shin
Corporation

Youth Media Council

Clear
Channel

Needs
Knowledge
Technology

Livelihoods
Corporate/Govt. Connections
Diversity of Opportuity

Values
Free Speech
Fairness in Reporting
Consumerism

Tools
Trade
Agree-
ment
Rules

World
Association
Christian
Communication

Campaign for
Popular Media
Reform

Thai Govt.

Tools
Mergers, Acquisitions
Joint Ventures, Cross Selling

US Govt.
NTIA
FCC

State of California

Resources

Ecumenical Statements

An Interfaith Statement on International Trade and Investment. Interfaith Working Group on Trade and Investment, 2001. Broad-based coalition of U.S. Protestant and Catholic organizations articulate five principles for trade and investment.

Religious/Ethical/ Human Rights Perspectives

Brubaker, Pamela K. *Globalization at What Price? Economic Change and Daily Life.* Cleveland: Pilgrim Press, 2001. A faith perspective on the realities of globalization and ways to make a difference.

International Human Rights Internship Program and Asian Forum for Human Rights and Development. *Training Manual on Economic, Social and Cultural Rights.* Washington, DC. A manual drawn from global experience on the substance and strategies to protect and promote economic, social, and cultural rights.

Peters, Rebecca Todd. *In Search of the Good Life—The Ethics of Globalization.* New York: The Continuum International Publishing Group, 2004. A Christian feminist ethicist gives globalization a human face and uncovers its moral assumptions in easy to understand language.

Putting Dignity & Rights at the Heart of the Global Economy: A Quaker Perspective. American Friends Service Committee, 2004. The results of a two-year consultation process examines trade, finance, and migration aspects of globalization and proposes actions for change.

Rifkin, Ira. *Spiritual Perspectives on Globalization—Making Sense of Economic and Cultural Upheaval.* Skylight Path Publishing, 2003. Explains globalization through the lens of eight different faith traditions.

Simon, Arthur. *How Much Is Enough? Hungering for God in an Affluent Culture.* Grand Rapids, Michigan: Baker Books, 2003. The founder of Bread for the World examines the faith imperative in the context of wealth and poverty, affluence, power, and consumerism.

Basic Guides to Understanding Globalization

Anderson, Sarah and John Cavanagh with Thea Lee. *Field Guide to the Global Economy.* Institute for Policy Studies, 2000. Explains the basic workings of the global economy in the language of ordinary people.

Anderson, Sarah and John Cavanagh. "Top 200: The Rise of Corporate Global Power." Institute for Policy Studies, December 2000, www.ips-dc.org/downloads/Top_200.pdf. Helps people get a grasp on how large many corporations are, and how they compare in resources to nation-states, with useful statistics.

Ellwood, Wayne. *The No-Nonsense Guide to Globalization.* No-Nonsense Guides, New Internationalist Publications, 2002. www.newint.org/shop/us/nonoglob.htm. Compact book explains history, major events, and realities that make up globalization around the world as well as some strategies for change, from a practical international justice perspective.

_____. "The Great Privatization Grab." *New Internationalist,* Issue 355, April 2003. www.newint.org. A very good picture of sale of public assets to private interests around the world, the scale of profits, and how it is happening.

Ransom, David and Anita Roddick. *No-Nonsense Guide to Fair Trade*. No-Nonsense Guides, New Internationalist Publications, 2002. www. newint.org/shop/us/nonofair.htm. Reveals the realities of trade as experienced by coffee growers in Central America or the workers making jeans in Bangladesh sweatshops, the roles played by the WTO, UNCTAD, ILO, IMF, G7, and other powerful organizations.

Rivoli, Pietra. *The Travels of a T-Shirt in the Global Economy*. John Wiley and Sons, 2005. Business professor takes the reader on a fascinating around-the-world adventure to reveal the life story of her six-dollar T-shirt, from a West Texas cotton field to a Chinese factory, and from trade negotiations in Washington to a used clothing market in Africa, revealing the complexities of international trade.

Seabrook, *Jeremy. No-Nonsense Guide to World Poverty*. No-Nonsense Guides, New Internationalist Publications, 2003. www.newint. org/shop/us/nonopoverty.htm. Drawing on testimonies from around the world, as well as on the hard facts, it challenges the assumption that wealth overcomes poverty, and demonstrates that the opposite of "poor" is not "rich" but "self-reliant."

General Books on Globalization from a Variety of Perspectives

Buchholz, Todd G. *Bringing the Jobs Home: How the Left Created the Outsourcing Crisis— and How We Can Fix It*. Sentinel Penguin Group, 2004. Former Bush economic policy advisor identifies failed anti-business government policies as the root cause of current economic problems.

Chua, Amy. *World on Fire: How Exploring Free Market Democracy Breeds Ethnic Hatred and Global Instability*. Doubleday, 2002. Examines the impact of globalization in each region on creation of ethnic elites and resulting civil strife.

Ehernreich, Barbara. *Nickled and Dimed—On (Not) Getting By in America*. New York: Metropolitan Books, 2001. The U.S. economy from the perspective of those on the bottom.

Friedman, Thomas L. *The Lexus and the Olive Tree*. Anchor Books, 2000. A columnist's look at the many aspects and realities of globalization and their meaning for the U.S.'s role in the world.

_____. *The World is Flat: A Brief History of the Twenty-first Century*. Farrar, Strauss and Giroux, 2005. Highly readable descriptions of some of globalization's major changes, the implications for the United States and other countries, and the corporations.

Kivel, Paul. *You Call This a Democracy? Who Benefits, Who Pays And Who Really Decides?* The Apex Press, 2004. A perspective on who controls economic and political power in the United States.

Lindsey, Brink. *Against the Dead Hand: The Uncertain Struggle for Global Capitalism*. John Wiley & Sons, 2001. A historical perspective on globalization that views the problem with globalization as the fact that market liberalization is still incomplete.

Mokhiber, Robert and Robert Weissman. *On the Rampage: Corporate Predators and the Destruction of Democracy*. Common Courage Press, 2005. Details the actions of multinational corporations around the world as well as resistance to theses activities.

Roby, Edward. "Globalization Spawns Wealth, But Not Equality as Deep Poverty Persists." *Asian Wall Street Journal*, January 19, 2005. http://www.questionsforthefuture.tv/ws1.

Soros, George. *On Globalization.* New York: Public Affairs, Perseus Books Group, 2002. Financial wizard and philanthropist Soros explains his view that global capitalism needs to become more stable and equitable, and his thoughts on how that can happen.

Source Watch. War Profiteering Center for Media and Democracy, May 2000. http://www.sourcewatch.org/index.php?title+War_profiteering. Compilation of reports of activities between U.S. corporations operating reconstruction activities in Iraq.

Lesson Plans, Participatory Exercise, Popular Education Materials

Bigelow, Bill and Bob Peterson, ed. *Rethinking Globalization—Teaching for Justice in an Unjust World.* Rethinking Schools, 2002. Excellent resource for participatory ways of teaching teenagers about globalization.

GlobalLocalPopEd, www.GlobalLocalPopEd.org. Website with resources and strategies for local work, profiles work of low income individuals and communities of color effected by globalization and their work on global justice.

Prokosch, Mike and Laura Raymond. *The Global Activists Manual: Local Ways to Change the World.* Thunder's Mouth Press/Nation Books, 2002. Follows heroes and heroines known and unknown, challenging the world's largest corporations. Includes protest photos, cartoons, and outrageous quotes.

Today's Globalization—Popular Education Tool Kit. Project South, 2005. www.projectsouth.org. Helpful tools for building a group understanding of globalization, its historical roots and local effects and what to do about it. Suitable for high school students and above.

"Trading Trainers Game." CAFOD (a UK Catholic development and relief agency). www.cafod.org.uk. A simulation game exploring the way unfair trade and unstable economies directly affect the lives of families in developing countries. Game for 15 to 40 people aged 13 and up.

United for a Fair Economy. www.faireconomy.org/econ. Downloadable workshops on FTAA, Globalization, Globalization for Beginners, Trainers' Resources, et al. Includes their own materials and those of many other organizations including the Women's Division.

Books and Other Resouces on Specific Topics

Resources

Armstrong, Franny. *Drowned Out.* Bullfrog Films. http://www.bullfrogfilms.com/catalog/child.html. Film tells the inspiring story of thousands of Indian villagers and their allies fighting the development of a dam that would result in the flooding of their homes and farms in the Narmada valley.

NOW with Bill Moyers: Leasing the Rain. PBS Frontline World. http://www.pbs.org/now/science/bolivia.html. Video portraying the Cochabamba, Bolivia struggle between citizen need and multinational corporation profits over water (75 minutes).

Olivera, Oscar with Tom Lewis. *Cochabamba! Water War In Bolivia.* South End Press, 2004. The story of the struggle against water and natural gas privatization in Bolivia.

The WASH Campaign: (Water, Sanitation, and Hygiene for All) www.wsscc.org. This advocacy campaign supports the United Nations Millennium Goal of halving the proportion of people without access to safe water and basic sanitation by 2015, and has been endorsed by the Women's Division.

Resources (continued)

"Water: Every Drop Counts." *New Internationalist*, Issue 354, March 2003. www.newint.org.

Livelihoods

A Fair Globalization: Creating Opportunities for All. World Commission on the Social Dimension of Globalization, International Labour Organization, 2004. http://www.ilo.org/public/english/wcsdg/docs/report.pdf. United Nations group that includes government, business, transnational corporations, labor, academia, and civil society and makes recommendations on how to expand the benefits of globalization with a focus on people, a democratic and effective state, and sustainable development.

Lewis, Avi and Naomi Klein. *The Take.* www.nfb.ca/thetake. A video portraying Argentina's economic collapse through the eyes of 30 unemployed auto-parts workers who walk into their idle factory and refuse to leave, work to restart the machines and seek to reclaim industrial jobs and democracy.

Where Are the Beans? Mennonite Central Committee. http://www.mcc.org/areaserv/latinamerica/honduras/resources.html. Excellent video tells the story of how globalization policies deprive Honduran farmers of their harvest. The accompanying study guide includes background information, study questions, recipes, advocacy suggestions, and a litany. Suitable for grades 5 and up (13 minutes).

Child Labor

One Child's Labor. 1996. Age level: middle school to adult. Chronicles the effort of thirteen-year-old Canadian Craig Kielburger, who began a global movement with other young people to address the problem of child labor (13 minutes, VHS). Pair this with the web-based study guide, *Caution: Children at Work!*

Caution: Children at Work! Church World Service. http://www.churchworldservice.org/childwrk. html. A brief web-based study/action guide exploring the necessity of work for some children under age 15, its often harmful consequences, and responses by people of faith to this very complex issue.

Rugmark, http://www.rugmark.org. The Rugmark website provides additional stories and ways to be in action to help end child labor.

Migration

Rivera, Alex. *The Sixth Section.* 2003. www.subcine.com/sixthsection.html. Cross-border organizing profiled as Mexican immigrants in New York raise money to rebuild their hometown in Mexico.

Global Media

The People's Communications Charter: An International Covenant of Standards and Rights. Center for Communications and Human Rights, Netherlands. Drafted by a group of organizations including the World Association of Christian Communications, the Charter affirms communications as a basic right and sets out standards for the protection of those rights.

Women

Bankrupt U.S. Economic Policy Forecloses on Women's Human Rights. Center of Concern, 2005. Report on the impacts of trade liberalization on women's human rights in the United States. Also deals with employment, privatization, access to service, agriculture, and food security.

Barndt, Deborah, ed. *Women Working The NAFTA Food Chain: Women, Food and Globalization.* Ontario: Second Story Press, 1999. How gender fits into the globalization picture. Relates the experience of women food system workers in the United States, Canada, and Mexico. Gives examples of women's alternatives.

Global Assembly Line. Church World Service, 1985. Video about working conditions of women workers in Mexico, the Philippines, and the United States. Originally funded partially by the Women's Division, the video is good for comparison with present realities (60 minutes, middle school to adult).

IGTN On-Line Learning Module: General Agreement on Trade in Service (GATS) IGTN– Asia. www.igtn.org/page/435. Coalition of women trade activists. Profiles women's trade issues in each region, with a major focus on WTO policies.

International Gender and Trade Network www.igtn.org. Global and regional gender perspectives on trade and economic literacy materials on issues such as health.

Peralta, Athena K. *A Caring Economy: A Feminist Contribution on the AGAPE.* World Council of Churches.

_____. *Women and Economic Globalization: A Discussion Paper.* World Council of Churches Programme on Women and Globalization, 2004. Religious community perspectives on the impact of globalization on women and the role of women in the neoliberal strategy.

Prowse, Joan, dir. *Women of Change.* Cinefocus Canada. This video tells the story of women organizing around welfare and workplace issues in Canada and Mexico (55 minutes). Order from Filmakers Library, New York, NY, www.filmakers.com.

Race, Gender and Ethnicity in the Dynamics of Poverty in Latin America and the Caribbean/ Género, Raza y Etnia en las Dinámicas de la Pobreza en América Latina y el Caribe. Articulacao de Mulheres Brasileiras, ActionAid Brasil, ActionAid International Americas, 2005. Racial

and ethnic women's perspectives on the connections and impacts of economic policies on women's identities.

Trading Away Our Rights: Women Working in Global Supply Chains. Make Trade Fair, Oxfam, February 2004. http://www.oxfam.org.uk/what_ we_do/issues/trade/trading_rights.htm. Good picture of globalization's women workers around the world and suggestions for action.

Alternatives

Across Race and Nation Project Reports. Southern Regional Council, Highlander Research and Education Center and the Center for Research on Women. Project exploring ways to build cross-race and cross-nationality coalitions in the south. Cross-racial collaboration examples and other materials available in English and Spanish from www.highlander center.org.

Alternatives to Economic Globalization (A Better World Is Possible): A Report of The International Forum on Globalization. International Forum on Globalization, 2002. www.ifg. org/programs/AltsBKPressRelease.pdf. A compilation of international activists' ideas about alternatives to present economic globalization, from a new global commons to alternatives to the World Bank.

Broad, Robin, ed. *Global Backlash Citizen Initiatives for a Just World Economy.* Rowman Littlefield Publishers, Inc., 2002. Examples from around the world of a wide variety of protests and alternative action on issues and policies.

Clark, John, ed. *Globalizing Civic Engagement: Civil Society and Transnational Action.* Earthscan Publications, 2003. www.earthscan. co.uk. Case studies of civil society organizations working internationally, including achievements and challenges.

Resources (continued)

Coop America's Supermarket Campaign. www.coopamerica.org. A way to encourage local supermarkets and other businesses to carry Fair Trade products.

Dare to Share, 1995. Age level: middle school to adult. Views the work of the One Great Hour of Sharing offering, through the eyes of two teenage girls, Kristen from the United States and Anna from Armenia. Shows programs that are making a difference in people's lives around the globe. Leaders guide included (11 minutes, VHS).

From Consumerism to Caring—25 Ways to Create a New Kind of Economy, Women's Division, General Board of Global Ministries, United Methodist Church, available from the Service Center, 1-800-305-9857. Action packet on a wide variety of globalization issues including food, sweatshops, and debt. Includes hymns, prayers, and litanies; video on World Trade Organization also available.

Global Poverty: From Despair to Solutions. 1989 Age level: high school to adult. This video profiles the Grameen Bank in Bangladesh, which has successfully pioneered providing small loans to women as a grassroots solution to poverty and hunger (18 minutes, VHS).

Longacre, Doris Janzen. *Living More with Less.* Herald Press, 1980. Provides practical suggestions for living with less from around the world, including money, clothing, homes, transportation and travel, celebrations, and recreation.

_____. *Living More with Less Cookbook.* Herald Press, 1976. Five hundred recipes from Mennonite kitchens for those who care about their own health and the food needs of others in the world, and how to eat better and consume less of the world's limited food resources.

New Initiatives for Sustainable Communities. 1999. Age level: high school to adult. This video examines how economic globalization is affecting small-scale farmers and rural people in Haiti, and community organizing efforts of the peasant movement (15 minutes, VHS).

New Internationalist magazine, http://www.newint.org. Monthly magazine that reports on issues of world poverty and inequality and highlights justice struggles. New topic each month: water, violence, women, etc.

Reclaim the Media—Media Reform Activist Toolkit. www.reclaimthemedia.org. Resource materials for action on media policy, media literacy education, and community media; includes samples of local government resolutions on media ownership diversity.

Solnit, David, ed. *Globalize Liberation: How to Uproot the System and Build a Better World.* San Francisco: City Lights Books, 2004. Weaves together the experiences and insights of community organizers, direct action movements, and global justice struggles from North America, Europe, and Latin America. Thirty-three essays provide food for thought, examples of effective action, and practical tools for everyone to use.

Weinbaum, Eve. *To Move a Mountain: Fighting the Global Economy in Appalachia.* New Press. www.newpress.com. Inspirational account of how a group of Appalachian men and women, affected by the disaster of local plant closings, became unlikely activists in the Tennessee statehouse and in the protests in Seattle against the World Trade Organization.

Resources in Both English and Spanish

Aguilar, Jose Victor and Miguel Cavada. *Free Trade—Free Reign for Transnational Corporations/Libe comercio…libertinaje des las trasna-

cionales. Ecumenical Program in Central America and the Caribbean, 2003.

_____. *Ten Plagues of Globalization/ 10 Plagas de la Globalizacion Neoliberal.* Ecumenical Program in Central America and the Caribbean, 2002. A fun way to learn about problems caused by globalization from a Salvadoran popular education perspective.

epicabooks@epica.org, www.epica.org. Central American and Caribbean popular education. Basic information on free trade and globalization translated for use by U.S. grassroots groups. Great cartoons.

Lewis, Anne and Fran Ansley. *Morristown Video Letters: Stories from the Grassroots About Globalization.* Available from www.highlandercenter.org. Workers affected by globalization in Tennessee, Mexico, and on the U.S./Mexico border offer a working class critique of globalization. Designed to be used a few segments at a time for discussion, education, and organizing (60 minutes).

Peredo Beltran, Elizabeth. *Water, Privatization and Conflict: The Women of Cochabamba Valley.* North America: Heinrich Boll Foundation, 2004. Description of the fundamental role of women in the struggle over privatization of water services in Cochabamba, Bolivia, in 2000.

Snitow, Alan and Deborah Kaufman. *Thirst.* 2004. www.thirstthemovie.org. Order from: www.bullfrogfilms.com. Video tells the stories of communities in Bolivia, India, and California who are battling corporate interests over the right to water. Includes Spanish, French, and Portuguese versions. Study guide available on website.

Uprooted: Refugees of the Global Economy, 2002. National Network for Immigrant and Refugee Rights, www.nnirr.org. Video portray-

ing three immigrants from Bolivia, Haiti, and the Philippines forced to leave their countries because of globalization, and their experiences with U.S. immigration policy.

Organizing and Organizations

Alliance for Responsible Trade, www.art-us.org. Washington, DC based advocacy coalition that partners with Fair Trade and other advocacy groups, particularly in North and South America.

Bread for the World. http://www.bread.org. A nationwide Christian citizens' movement seeking justice for the world's hungry people by lobbying our nation's decision makers. A good way to keep up with pending legislation and read background information on issues such as food stamps, the minimum wage, international debt relief, and the Special Supplemental Nutrition Program for Women, Infants, and Children (WIC).

Center for Media and Democracy. http://www.imf.org/external/pubs/ft/fandd/2002/03/picture.htm. Non-profit organization that works to strengthen democracy by promoting media that are "of, by, and for the people." Produces a quarterly investigative journal, *Spin of the Day*, which offers daily reporting on spin and propaganda in the news; and *SourceWatch*, a wiki-based investigative journalism resource to which anyone can contribute.

Christian Aid. www.christianaid.org.uk/worship. An international development assistance agency of the churches in the UK and Ireland. Includes prayers, reflection, church magazine articles, and information on economic impacts and strategies worldwide.

Clean Clothes Campaign. www.cleanclothes.org. Global coalition that works to improve the working conditions of garment workers worldwide, providing consumers with information about how their garments are produced and advocacy strategies to assist workers.

Ecumenical Advocacy Alliance, World Council of Churches www.e-alliance.ch/trade.jsp. Sponsors Global Week of Action on Trade, a yearly global campaign of advocacy, action, and media strategies to impact the lives of the world's poorest people through action on trade that can be used by local groups. Also an excellent source of stories on trade justice and injustice, as well as worship resources on trade.

Global Envision. http://www.globalenvision. org/library/4/575/. The organization's goal is to ensure that the poor are not left behind by globalization, and that technology be a tool that local people in the developing world can use to take advantage of opportunities, instead of being taken advantage of with this tool.

Global Exchange. http://www.globalexchange. org. An international human rights organization dedicated to promoting environmental, political, and social justice. Areas of work include fair trade, war and peace, sweatshops, WTO, IMF/World Bank, and FTAA.

@Grassroots.org. http://www.grass-roots.org/ index.shtml. Tells the stories of the most innovative grassroots programs in the United States and the local heroes who've found effective ways to build their communities, fix what's broken, and make them better.

Interfaith Trade Justice Campaign, www. tradejusticeusa.org. Trade basics workshop, bulletin inserts. This coalition of religious groups working on trade prepares a wide variety of materials for use by local groups wishing to learn about and be active on trade. Mobilizes and facilitates an active engagement of faith communities in educational activities, policy advocacy, and fair trade.

Addresses a variety of trade issues efforts and ways to take action.

Institute for Agriculture and Trade Policy. www. iatp.org. Minnesota-based research and advocacy organization that is a source of good information on the impact of economic policies on U.S. farmers.

Oxfam International: Make Trade Fair Campaign. www.maketradefair.com. Educational materials on a variety of trade issues and commodities, such as coffee, chocolate, corn, and bananas; fair trade by country, campaign ideas, etc.

Peoples' Consultation on FTAA Hemispheric Social Alliance. www.peoplesconsultation.org. A coalition of citizens' organizations advocating on trade and other economic issues. Produces educational materials for teachers and parents and resources for organizing.

Public Citizen. http://www.citizen.org/cmep/ Water/cmep_Water/reports/. A Washington, DC based advocacy group promoting a sustainable future through clean energy, safe food, and water for all. http://www.citizen.org/ index.cfm. Reports from around the world chronicle grassroots efforts on water.

Tradecraft. www.traidcraft.co.uk. A Christian effort to fight poverty through trade. A fair trading company exchange works with poor people to help get their fair share of world trade. Includes resources for speakers and trade facts.

Women's Edge Coalition. http://www.womens edge.org/pages/aboutus/index.jsp. Forty organizational members and over 15,000 individual members nationwide. Provides focused, practical advocacy to make sure that U.S. international trade and assistance programs create economic opportunities and self-sufficiency for women and their families worldwide.

Author

elmira Nazombe is a Co-Executive Secretary for Racial Justice of the Women's Division, responsible for assisting United Methodist Women through the development of advocacy strategies and biblical and theological reflection materials on racial justice. She has worked in the areas of social and economic justice and human rights for over four decades. She served as Director of Leadership Development and Global Education for the Center for Women's Global Leadership at Rutgers University from 1998-2004 and Director of the Office of International Justice and Human Rights for Church World Service, NCCCUSA between 1994 and 1998. She has worked for several ecumenical agencies, including the All Africa Conference of Churches and the National Christian Council of Kenya. She trained as both an educator and an urban planner.

elmira has been active over the last 15 years as a popular educator, particularly in workshops and production of materials on the gender impacts of globalization. She is a doctoral candidate in Social and Philosophical Foundations of Education at Rutgers University, focusing on how women use education methodologies to work for social and economic transformation. She lives in Highland Park, New Jersey, with her adult son.

Memo

Memo

Memo

Memo

The Big G—Mission Study on Globalization: Youth Book with Leader's Guide

By Tamara Walker

(#3725) $6.00

There is evidence of the Big G all around you. When you're shopping at Wal-Mart and you notice that almost everything you see on the racks is made in China. When you're placing a long-distance call and find that the person assisting you is speaking from India. When you notice that the textile workers at the factory in your town all seem to be immigrant women. The book provides creative approaches, adaptable to church school, youth group, or retreat setting, to help youth deal with the pervasive nature of globalization, and deal with its implications for their lives and the lives of young people around the world.

Please mail order with check payable to:

SERVICE CENTER
GENERAL BOARD OF GLOBAL MINISTRIES
7820 READING RD CALLER NO 1800
CINCINNATI OH 45222-1800

Costs for shipping and handling:

SALE ITEMS:
$25 or less, add $5.35
$25.01– $60, add $6.65
$60.01– $100, add $8.05
Over $100, add 8.5%

FREE ITEMS:
50 or less, add $4.05
51– 400, add $5.20
Over 400, add $1.75 per 100

If billing is preferred, a $2.00 billing fee is charged in addition to shipping and handling.

For billed or credit card orders:

WEBSITE: www.scorders.org
E-MAIL: scorders@gbgm-umc.org
CALL TOLL-FREE: 1-800-305-9857
FAX ORDERS: 1-513-761-3722